Routledge Revivals

On the Poetry of Spenser and the Form of Romances

Originally published in 1956, this scholarly study of Spenser's poetry shows how the conceptions of his earlier work in complaints, visions and pastorals were of continuing importance to the development of *The Faerie Queene*. Following on from Bishop Hurd's Letters on Chivalry and Romance, John Arthos discusses the congeniality of romance and allegory. The form and substance of Spenser's lyrical and meditative poetry were combined with his interest in romances to govern the progress of the great work, and in the *Mutabilitie Cantos* they assert a dominant emphasis. In continuing many of the features characteristic of medieval romances, in taking up the innovations of Boiardo and Ariosto, and in giving expression to a view of life and especially of love that had not been made before in romantic literature, Spenser set himself a framework of so many and such complex interests that he failed to construct in *The Faerie Queene* the unity one might expect after reading the letter to Raleigh. The author believes that Tasso's theories provide the terms that explain how Spenser meant to effect the unity of his poem, and that they also explain why the *Mutabilitie Cantos* belong to a radically different conception. Acknowledging that the allegories in Spenser's work are obscure or unevenly developed John Arthos' book maintains the idea that romance and allegory were integrally conceived in the Poem.

On the Poetry of Spenser and the Form of Romances

John Arthos

First published in 1956 by George Allen & Unwin Ltd

This edition first published in 2024 by Routledge
4 Park Square, Milton Park, Abingdon, Oxon, OX14 4RN
and by Routledge
605 Third Avenue, New York, NY 10158.

Routledge is an imprint of the Taylor & Francis Group, an informa business

ISBN 13: 978-1-032-83319-4 (hbk)
ISBN 13: 978-1-003-50892-2 (ebk)
ISBN 13: 978-1-032-83357-6 (pbk)
Book DOI 10.4324/9781003508922

On the Poetry of Spenser and the Form of Romances

JOHN ARTHOS

GEORGE ALLEN & UNWIN LTD
RUSKIN HOUSE
MUSEUM STREET LONDON

FIRST PUBLISHED IN 1956

PRINTED IN GREAT BRITAIN

in 12 point Bembo type

BY UNWIN BROTHERS LIMITED

WOKING AND LONDON

To

M. E. A.

χρύσιον ἦλθες

PREFACE

As the reader of Spenser sees the range of his achievement, he comes to think of these poems as the various and extensive work of a mind that is always trying itself out, and that is always sure of its mastery of form and art. It is this as much as anything that gives the question of the unity of *The Faerie Queene* its interest, the thought that here also there must have been an assured conception when all the rest is so perfectly managed.

The subjects of *The Faerie Queene* from book to book show what we are to accept as the ways of life of a gentleman—humility before God, temperance, the integrity of love, loyalty to law and to humanity. Whether or not there is progression in the unfolding of such matters one would suppose Spenser meant to devise a structure for his theme that would support both the singleness and the complexity of the idea. But the work is unfinished, the letter to Raleigh is hard to square with the poem we have, the books are written in somewhat different patterns, and, most strangely of all, the allegories are so variously or at times obscurely or unevenly developed that the reader finds it difficult to discover the point of view from which he is expected to take it all in.

Part of the difficulty is surely the modern reader's as much as the Elizabethan writer's confusion about allegory generally, and part was pointed out by Bishop Hurd in his *Letters on Chivalry and Romance* when he argued that Spenser's poem should be judged by "Gothic" rather than classic ideas of unity. I think it is true that our understanding of *The Faerie Queene* is improved when we compare it with some other romance writing, and indeed the present study takes up again from Bishop Hurd. I have given some attention to the congeniality of romance and allegory in the persuasion that Spenser in *The Faerie Queene* was not trying to marry two or more forms according to some interest of his judgment, and to support the idea that all was integrally conceived. If what follows helps to confirm this, other questions affecting the uses and methods of allegory can be more easily answered.

I am conscious of many more obligations to Spenser scholars than are indicated in the notes, and so here I should like to acknowledge my indebtedness over the years to the writings of C. H. Herford, Edwin Greenlaw, W. L. Renwick, and C. S. Lewis especially. In other ways I want to express my obligations to Sergio Baldi, H. T. Price, and the late Albert Pauphilet.

The writing of this study was substantially done in Florence in 1949 and 1950 when I held a Fulbright research fellowship at the University there, a grant I was able to accept through the award of a sabbatical leave from the University of Michigan. Publication has been aided by the Horace H. Rackham School of Graduate Studies.

J. A.

CONTENTS

The Beginning

The Faerie Queene begins with the variety and complexity of life. The journey of one knight through vast forests in a strange land is followed by similar journeys of other knights into innumerable vicissitudes, and all is not merely a succession of events, for they are ordered to show in what complexity man moves as he moves towards his perfection. So much in the world is not what it seems, so much that might seem well disposed is bitterly hostile, and to match the endlessness of illusion and deceit there are endless efforts for glory and love, and there are also the gifts of grace.

It is in the sense of the fecundity of good and evil, in the abundance of life, that Spenser contrives his knights' adventures, and what guides them in their hope of bringing order and justice for a while to the world, slaying a dragon, freeing a maiden, must also guide him in presenting this rich and various world as all of a piece, something for all its variety as intelligibly fitting into the scheme of things. As an artist and as a man who shares the goals of his protagonists he must make of all this vast activity a poem.

He must because the variety and richness of life at the beginning gave him his first great occasion. *The Shepheardes Calender*, the different poems for twelve months, their different metres, the range of subject, signify in every way the variety in the succession of things. And there also began somewhere in the complaints of Colin in these poems or in the translations of the *Regrets* and *Visions* of Du Bellay and Petrarch the expression of what finally took form in a poem that means to show how man attains glory.

In the early poems as in the greatest work individuals in the midst of the variety of things will define the desires that move the poet, and the fulfilment he can accept. From beginning to end the lyrical poet, the personal interpreter, is in harmony with the questing figures of his imagination, Colin, Cuddie, St. George, and their satisfaction and completion is his. There were difficulties in finding the methods of expression, for all such identifications, and how important the search for form was is clear enough not merely in the self-conscious remarks on the pastoral convention that begin *The Shepheardes Calender*, but even more obviously in the lines that introduce *The Faerie Queene* where Spenser, only partly in a conventionally humble way, remarks on the shift from pastoral to heroic poetry and where, consistently enough, the language does not mention the forms of the poems but the guise of the poet. Till then he has been posing as a shepherd singing to his friends and to a shepherdess, but now, opening the romantic poem, he speaks of himself as a minstrel used to singing warlike deeds to companies of knights and ladies. There are many reasons that serve his beginning *The Faerie Queene* this way, the memory of Boiardo at Scandiano and Ariosto at Ferrara, and some derived memory, perhaps, of the *Song of Roland* as well as the clearest signal from the beginning of the *Aeneid*. In the new role the matter of the poetry is changed, but there will continue the emphasis upon the singer that will give a final character even to so complex a work as *The Faerie Queene*, the whole continuously presented as the vision of one singer. As if, in the form of the romantic narrative, Spenser had found what would give his individuality its greatest scope.

It is rather curious that in all his other poetry that survives there are no stories of chivalry or adventure that offer us the chance to say, here is an early sketch of *The Faerie Queene*. There are no poems, as in Chaucer there are poems and stories that help foretell *Troilus and Criseyde*, and there is nothing like a *Rinaldo* to become in due time the *Gerusalemme Liberata*.[1] Nevertheless, in Spenser's

[1] It has been well observed, however, that Tasso's efforts to find his own beginning form in the romance showed him that his strength must be given eventually to other kinds of writing. "Il *Rinaldo* invece sta a dimostrare che il libro delle mirabili avventure dei cavalieri era ormai chiuso per lui: come scialbe e insignificanti le imprese guerresche dei suoi eroi! come povera la storia dei loro amori! Se quella materia si era offerta al giovane poeta, desideroso di provare le proprie forze, come la più familiare e la più ovvia, tutti i dodici canti, stesi con tanta franchezza, ma privi o quasi di accenti fortemente personali,

numerous poems that came before *The Faerie Queene* there is something of its substance, and there is much to help us (with hindsight) to foretell the nature and quality of the form he was finally attracted to. The terms that can guide us are simple enough to begin with—pastoral, complaint, vision—and as one sees the conventions they point to, mingled and developed in his constantly richer and more complex music, one begins to see how the form of the romance shares in that original lyrical enterprise, and how stories of questing knights might be seen to belong with poems about the months.

The note of humbleness is held faithfully and naturally in each poem of *The Shepheardes Calender* as if it were the inevitable subject of all twelve. The dialect in part, the simple talk about feeding sheep and cutting down trees and doing one's proper work, and the talk about putting up with life and enduring it somehow—all this is faithful to the note of plainness, which yet exists primarily in something else, in the characters themselves and particularly in Colin. The views, the thoughts are never grand or magnificent, for everywhere there is the consciousness of the simplicity of the shepherd, which here appears to be in part a simplicity of character and understanding Spenser supposes so far to be his own, and in part it appears to present a purity and humility he wishes to attain, and as a poet to express.

There is everywhere the confession of humbleness and the note of plain people, Willie, Thenot, Cuddie, Rosalind. They speak neither with the learned beauty nor the sense of cultivation that belong to Virgil's and Milton's shepherds, but as people who are

ci dicono che il Tasso non ha trovato in quella materia la *sua* materia, in quell'ambiente cavalleresco, l'ambiente della sua poesia.

"Perché la caratteristica prima del *Rinaldo* è, direi, la sua provvisorietà: tutto è provvisorio in questo poema, la trama che potrebbe essere anche diversa —e bene ha dimostrato l'inconsistenza dell'intreccio e la debolezza di tutta l'opera il Mazzoni nel suo limpido studio, i cui risultati sono da tempo ormai acquisiti tutti dalla critica,—i caratteri dei personaggi, l'espressione, il ritmo." (Mario Fubini, "Il 'Rinaldo' del Tasso," in *Studi sulla Letteratura del Rinascimento*, Florence: Sansoni, 1947, pp. 215–16. Mazzoni's essay is printed in the preliminary pages of A. Solerti's edition of the *Opere minori in versi* of Tasso, Vol. I, Bologna, 1891.)

almost unsophisticated, who fall in love, who make poems, who are on the side of honesty, and who have heard that once upon a time the world went more smoothly—

> They sayne the world is much war then it wont.
>
> (*September*, 108)

And so the first poem begins with Colin Cloute's description of himself,

> A Shepeheards boye (no better doe him call).
>
> (*Januarye*, 1)

The familiarity of the scene, when the setting exists so to speak at all, adds to the air of plainness, and for this, too, the landscape is something different from Virgil's or Ronsard's or Tasso's—

> Here has the salt Medway his sourse,
> wherein the Nymphes doe bathe.
> The salt Medway, that trickling stremis
> adowne the dales of Kent:
> Till with his elder brother Themis
> his brackish waues be meynt.
>
> (*Julye*, 79–84)

There is more, here, of the manner of Theocritus where the language modifies the elaborate pictures in an almost rough and homely way and especially in the unlocalized scenes:

> Ah for pittie, wil rancke Winters rage,
> These bitter blasts neuer ginne tasswage?
> The kene cold blowes through my beaten hyde,
> All as I were through the body gryde.
> My ragged rontes all shiver and shake,
> As doen high Towers in an earthquake:
> They wont in the wind wagge their wrigle tailes,
> Perke as Peacock: but nowe it auales.
>
> (*Februarie*, 1–8)

Even in Spring and Summer when beauty ennobles all, the world is still the world we all know and in the praise of its beauty there is everywhere restraint. If the scene at times admits the Graces and suggests the Elysian Fields one observes nevertheless the absence of the gods, beings one is disposed to welcome in such poetry:

> I neuer lyst presume to *Parnasse* hyll,
> But pyping lowe in shade of lowly groue,
> I play to please my selfe, all be it ill.
>
> (*June*, 70–2)

And in the marvellous stanzas of the April eclogue the restraint still holds, Muses come upon the scene to adorn Eliza, but not the gods: the Sun and Moon are brought to the mind's eye to compare with her beauty, but here as in the great dancing scene in the Pastorella episode of *The Faerie Queene* Nymphs and Graces dance for the lady, not goddesses. The offerings are the offerings of shepherds' daughters:

> Bring hether the Pincke and purple Cullambine,
> With Gelliflowres:
> Bring coronations, and Sops in wine,
> worne of Paramoures.
> Strowe me the ground with Daffadowndillies,
> And Cowslips, and Kingcups, and loued Lillies:
> The pretie Pawnce,
> And the Cheuisaunce,
> Shall match with the fayre flowre Delice.
>
> (*Aprill*, 136–44)

Spenser keeps back from the divine, and if he allows himself from time to time a reference to Pan or some other he only names the gods, he does not bring them forth, except Cupid once and even then "the little God" was scarcely seen:

> I bent my bolt against the bush,
> Listening if any thing did rushe,
> But then heard no more rustling.
> Tho peeping close into the thicke,
> Might see the mouing of some quicke,
> Whose shape appeared not:

But were it faerie, feend, or snake,
My courage earnd it to awake,
  And manfully thereat shotte.
With that sprong forth a naked swayne,
With spotted winges like Peacocks trayne,
  And laughing lope to a tree.
His gylden quiuer at his backe,
And siluer bowe, which was but slacke,
  Which lightly he bent at me.

(*March*, 70–84)

The interest in simplicity is communicated in its last emphasis indirectly, for these are poems which from the first are presented as works of art, marvellously complex, not merely in the diction and verse and rhetoric and the variety of subject but in the very idea of simplification. Mostly these shepherds appear to us not as coarse humanity and not as courtiers, but as beings who are simplified partly according to some sense of decorum and the picturesque, and partly according to the desired simplicity of the heart. Colin, in the first eclogue, complains, and in the finality of his grief breaks his pipe and throws himself on the ground. The gestures, the expressions are appropriate, and all, or almost all, is in the gesture, the shepherd who is not a shepherd although he is called one, but whose life like theirs is taken up with only a few things, whose grief exists chiefly in the (appropriate) signs, like one of those late Renaissance garden sculptures that cannot afford passion.

There is here nothing that is false, and were it not for the skill of the verse and the pleasure of observing the picturesquely simple, there would be little to hold the mind, chiefly the style, and the fashion that somehow charms us, thinking of the disconsolate lover as a shepherd. Nothing false, and nothing quite true, either to love or grief, and chiefly something interesting and even charming in the posing:

I loue thilke lasse, (alas why doe I loue?)
And am forlorne, (alas why am I lorne?)

(*Januarye*, 61–2)

Occasionally, as with *Februarie* at first, something comes close to our feelings, something clear and strong in the language raises an expectation of direct concern:

> Ah for pittie, wil rancke Winters rage,
> These bitter blasts neuer ginne tasswage?
>
> (1–2)

But the directness is deceptive, there is nothing so sharp and fearful as

> When icicles hang by the wall,
>   And Dick the shepherd blows his nail,
> And Tom bears logs into the hall,
>   And milk comes frozen home in pail.

There is too much alliteration for that, too formal a dignity to "rancke Winter" and "bitter blasts," too much forethought in an expression about standing against the wind like towers against an earthquake. The picture is clear, strong even, and grotesque, and as it happens this is such a mode for the grotesque that it pleases, and the image of the ugliness and cruelty of winter lacks the power to move.

Then, in the same poem, as the dialogue gets under way, and there is the story about the oak and the envious briar, what might appear at first to be simplicity itself, the proverbs and the proverbial rhetoric, is soon known to be something quite different, a most skilful transformation of a ruder teaching:

> The soueraigne of seas he blames in vaine,
> That once seabeate, will to sea againe.
>
> (33–4)
>
> His bared boughes were beaten with stormes,
> His toppe was bald, and wasted with wormes,
> His honor decayed, his braunches sere.
>
> (112–14)

The accent, the language, the dialect, the use of the colloquial give the situation weight and meaning and they support the narrative so that it never loses its balance as it both entertains and teaches, the story and the moral quite happy together. The people's wisdom, in short, is here rather elegantly adorned, although the truth and something of the simplicity of the story remain.

This is the joy of display and art, wit and imagination and verse expanding the plainness of the fable, and only once does anything like the proverb's rhetoric attempt to carry sentiment, that line with its genuine sadness—

> All that is lent to loue, wyll be lost.
>
> (70)

But here, too, however genuine, the sadness is the sadness of youth and of literature, without terror. More often in the earlier eclogues it is the art that is interesting, its elaborateness, its skill, its grace. Sometimes a narrative will be told so well we forget to admire the skill, but more frequently we are expected to find our pleasure in the gestures, in the conventions, in the simplification, and then, if we can, in the idea of pastoral simplicity.

In still other eclogues the art is made into a game, and the air of sport, of gaiety, of the artifice of life is as it were the content of the poem. In *March* Willye and Thomalyn are not so much talking about love as they are passing time wittily. What is especially charming is that this is the gaiety of young people, playing a game and telling a story of their own invention, no scruples or falseness of pretension, the fancy free of all control except the control of wit, itself ignorant of anything bitter—the *jeu d'esprit.*

> It was vpon a holiday,
> When shepheardes groomes han leaue to playe,
> I cast to goe a shooting.
> Long wandring vp and downe the land,
> With bowe and bolts in either hand,
> For birds in bushes tooting:
> At length within an Yuie todde
> (There shrouded was the little God)
> I heard a busie bustling.
>
> (61–9)

The art is elaborate, the pleasure in itself is gentle although the delight in the art is charming, but nothing approaches sentiment. So, too, in *Aprill* and *August*, one with songs about flowers, tuned "vnto the Waters fall," where almost nothing that is said and not even the pictures are so important as the movement of the verse itself: the other a rhyme-capping game so musical and high-spirited that the outrageous is delightful:

> And if for gracelesse greefe I dye,
>   hey ho gracelesse griefe,
> Witnesse, shee slewe me with her eye:
>   let thy follye be the priefe. (113–16)

If, then, these are poems where the manner is everything, or almost everything, there are some others in which the substance is more important, especially the *Maye* and *Julye* and *September* eclogues, where the ambitions and luxuries of some of the clergy are attacked. In these, too, the manner has its special interest and above all its special function—it allows for a concealed attack, the shepherds on the surface are talking only about shepherds, although we understand that there is some cleverness in the way the poet lets us know they are really talking about the pastors of Christian congregations. The pastoral device is being exploited and at every moment we have this in our minds. These eclogues, accordingly, are not to be regarded primarily as allegorical poems of the sort in which the concealed meaning is more absorbing than the surface story, and there is no such denseness of allusion that all the matters mentioned are to be taken in two ways. Sometimes the allegory for a moment is complete—

> The brethren twelue, that kept yfere
>   the flockes of mighty *Pan*—
> (*Julye*, 143–4)

although rather more often the allusion needs separate explanation—

> Diggon, I praye thee speake not so dirke.
> Such myster saying me seemeth to mirke.
> (*September*, 102–3)

Then, the point of the fox and kid story in the *Maye* eclogue, about a clever fox deceiving a simple kid, hardly serves the elaborate introduction on the evils of the Roman Catholic Church. For whatever reason the fable in itself is more interesting than that particular application of it.

Nevertheless, in these poems the relationship between one and the other meaning, and complaints about lazy shepherds and about careless clergymen, are a point the reader must be intent on, and it is in part from this that these eclogues belong with the others in the collection, for the display of art. Here, too, there is another kind of simplification, of character and feeling and idea, and the only difference is that by the nature of the subject we take the meaning a little more seriously than in some of the love complaints, we share more immediately in the statements, because, I suppose, the subject involves our ordinary responsibilities, but again, the satire is not deeply moving.

In one eclogue, though, the conventions are used for the expression of passion. The shepherds in *October*, here as members of an ancient but decayed world, by their dress and customs are clearly closer than some of the others to the world the gods once visited, and it is therefore fitting that divine inspiration should be something known and realized. In all pastoral poetry persons presented in the simplified form of the shepherds of a more innocent age, and whose lives are so much given to love and the complaints of love, are expected to affirm that love is the inspiration of divinity. And here as Piers speaks thus of Cuddie, the note of earnestness and exaltation is struck:

> Ah fon, for loue does teach him climbe so hie,
> And lyftes him vp out of the loathsome myre:
> Such immortall mirrhor, as he doth admire,
> Would rayse ones mynd aboue the starry skie.
> And cause a caytiue corage to aspire,
> For lofty loue doth loath a lowly eye.
>
> (91–6)

Cuddie in his turn says that love is divine but so furious in its raging that the poet under its power can no longer serve the Muses:

> All otherwise the state of Poet stands,
> For lordly loue is such a Tyranne fell:
> That where he rules, all power he doth expell.
> That vaunted verse a vacant head demaundes,
> Ne wont with crabbed care the Muses dwell.
> Vnwisely weaues, that takes two webbes in hand.
> (97–102)

The seriousness here brings the character of Spenser himself forward, not merely in his role as a shepherd, but with something of the clangor of ambition, expressing the knowledge he has that the mastery of an art can be put to other and greater uses. Even so, the poem ends quickly and there is no other chance for any intensity of expression that can match the intensity of the same confession in the *Hymns*.

If, then, the charm of Spring, of flowers, of love, and in the *October* eclogue some sense of the divinity of poetry lend a power to these poems that is not simply the poetry of humbleness, they add without transforming that essential quality. From the circumstances of each poem it could hardly be otherwise: a lover talking to himself, a young shepherd showing off before an old one, two young shepherds matching rhymes. All the poems are monologues or dialogues, and most frequently there is a recital, a simple performance by one speaker. *Januarye* is typical: a shepherd, described at first by the poet, complains of his unfortunate love. And at the beginning of the last poem there is the little introduction, "This Æglogue (euen as the first beganne) is ended with a complaynte of Colin to God Pan," and the description begins:

> The gentle shepheard satte beside a springe,
> All in the shadowe of a bushye brere,
> That *Colin* hight, which wel could pype and singe,
> For he of *Tityrus* his songs did lere.
> There as he satte in secreate shade alone,
> Thus gan he make of loue his piteous mone.
> (*December*, 1–6)

The beginning and the ending image is the single figure, the simple shepherd quite alone, in no defined scene except the scene of winter weather, talking or singing to himself. Again and again in the *Eclogues* there is the time when, even in a debate, the light turns on the solitary poet:

> Nought weigh I, who my song doth prayse or blame,
> Ne striue to winne renowne, or passe the rest:
> With shepheard sittes not, followe flying fame:
> But feede his flocke in fields, where falls hem best.
> I wote my rymes bene rough, and rudely drest:
> The fitter they, my carefull case to frame:
> Enough is me to paint out my vnrest,
> And poore my piteous plaints out in the same.
>
> (*June*, 73–80)

The figure is, of course, some shepherd-poet, who knows that times were better once, someone Spenser lets represent himself, for there is a serious interest and need Spenser has for the complaint of fortune, of the power of change in life, of the cruelty of the mistress who does not return love. But if Colin or Cuddie or whoever any more than the Red Crosse Knight is not exactly Spenser, this at least is true, that the monologue of the isolated figure, the picture of a man complaining is ever the controlling form of his poetry. At the beginning it controls the conventions and the substance of *The Shepheardes Calender*, as later it controls the *Mutabilitie* cantos. Where the poems are about two or three—Thomalin and Willye, or Willye and Perigot and Cuddie—there may be, as once, a kind of game, the sport of capping rhymes, but even in these there is likely to be the occasion for one to tell a story: a story about an upstart briar, or a foolish kid and a clever fox, stories in which the young are arrogant and the old are wise, or an incident about a shepherd who lets his flock be wasted. These will usually turn on some point of complaint, something that has gone wrong, so that in these, too, the attitude of one of the characters will be the central one, Thenot talking about the foolishness of youth, Colin telling about the loss of Rosalind, Cuddie complaining of the contempt of poetry—all common enough matters and all quite simply told about, and all turning our attention to the single figure, the individual man who is trying for all his disappointments to see life as a whole.

The separate parts of *The Shepheardes Calender*, the different incidents about shepherds and their loves in the world of changing seasons, are all true to a single conception of life, of a life where men do their daily tasks, fall in love, follow honesty and religion, decline before time and change, for all belongs to a single conception that gives the plainness, the dialect, the homely detail its force and sharpness and its poetry, a conception of simplicity and innocence at the heart of life. This is perhaps most clearly said in the *June* pastoral:

> Lo *Colin*, here the place, whose pleasaunt syte
> From other shades hath weand my wandring mynde.
> Tell me, what wants me here, to worke delyte?
> The simple ayre, the gentle warbling wynde,
> So calme, so coole, as no where else I fynde:
> The grassye ground with daintye Daysies dight,
> The Bramble bush, where Byrds of euery kynde
> To the waters fall their tunes attemper right.
>
> (1–8)

And Colin calls just this Paradise, and not some distant Elysian Field:

> O happy *Hobbinoll*, I blesse thy state,
> That Paradise hast found, whych *Adam* lost.
> Here wander may thy flock early or late,
> Withouten dreade of Wolues to bene ytost:
> Thy louely layes here mayst thou freely boste.
>
> (9–13)

In their own valleys, Hobbinol says, are the familiar divinities of their common life:

> Then if by me thou list aduised be,
> Forsake the soyle, that so doth the bewitch:
> Leaue me those hilles, where harbrough nis to see,
> Nor holybush, nor brere, nor winding witche:

And to the dales resort, where shepheards ritch,
And fruictfull flocks bene euery where to see.
Here no night Rauens lodge more black then pitche,
Nor eluish ghosts, nor gastly owles doe flee.

But frendly Faeries, met with many Graces,
And lightfote Nymphes can chace the lingring night,
With Heydeguyes, and trimly trodden traces,
Whilst systers nyne, which dwell on *Parnasse* hight,

Doe make them musick, for their more delight:
And *Pan* himselfe to kisse their christall faces,
Will pype and daunce, when *Phœbe* shineth bright:
Such pierlesse pleasures haue we in these places.
(17–32)

It is such a world, its beauty and variety, and its loss, that is the world of *The Shepheardes Calender*, the world seen beautifully and simply,

when all is ycladd
With pleasaunce: the grownd with grasse, the Woods
With greene leaues, the bushes with bloosming Buds.
(*Maye*, 6–8)

And when the poems are sad it is because this is the world Colin has lost. When that sadness is to be given its rein this or that poem turns into a complaint, and then it is that the solitary singer has his chance to bring feeling into his poetry, in lamenting the passing of the perfection that once belonged to the pastoral world:

And I, whylst youth and course of carelesse yeeres
Did let me walke withouten lincks of loue,
In such delights did ioy amongst my peeres . . .

Tho couth I sing of loue, and tune my pype
Vnto my plaintiue pleas in verses made:
Tho would I seeke for Queene apples vnrype,
To giue my *Rosalind*, and in Sommer shade

Dight gaudy Girlonds, was my comen trade,
To crowne her golden locks, but yeeres more rype,
And losse of her, whose loue as lyfe I wayd,
Those weary wanton toyes away did wype.
(*June*, 33–5, 41–8)

And there remains finally for Colin only such sad comfort as this,

Enough is me to paint out my vnrest.
(79)

The complaint is the complaint of lost perfection, and so it is that the pastoral, and the loss of the golden age that that convention by its nature signifies, is the preparation for it. And the role of the one who complains will always be with Spenser as an initial role, and as the beginning of his wisdom. At times, of course, he gives as it were to himself the command to assume another role and another work, as Piers, for example, in *October* advises Cuddie:

Abandon then the base and viler clowne,
Lyft vp thy selfe out of the lowly dust:
And sing of bloody Mars, of wars, of giusts,
Turne thee to those, that weld the awful crowne.
(37–40)

And at the beginning of *The Faerie Queene* Spenser proposes just such a change for himself:

Lo I the man, whose Muse whilome did maske,
  As time her taught, in lowly Shepheards weeds,
  Am now enforst a far vnfitter taske,
  For trumpets sterne to chaunge mine Oaten reeds,
  And sing of Knights and Ladies gentle deeds.

Instead of the innocent past the world of his poetry will now become the world of glory, and by necessity, by the urgency of his nature:

The noble hart, that harbours vertuous thought,
And is with child of glorious great intent,
Can neuer rest, vntill it forth haue brought
Th' eternall brood of glorie excellent.
(*F. Q.* I. v. 1)

But the poem will not be written down as from a Muse giving Homer words to describe the exploits of Achilles. The poem will take its words from the singer himself, the poet who accompanies the figures of his poem in each adventure as the figures of his own imagination and of his own needs. He himself will always be present in the poem, in the characters whose wagers are also his, and in his own person, he is beside them to intervene always when there is no longer need for a masque:

O that great Sabbaoth God, graunt me that Sabaoths sight.
(VII. viii. 2)

He is as much alone, as much the solitary singer in *The Faerie Queene*, as the piper in Arcadia, singing his unrest and his complaint. Only here he has made for himself the chance for profundity and conviction, the scope to explain the power of the dream of a life of glory.

Again and again in the short poems there is the one idea, the world has let the poet down, love is dead, poetry unhonoured, virtue is failing in the court and in the world, instability rules all. The same ideas, sometimes said flatly, sometimes in the form of fable or something like satire, and, interestingly enough, except for the fable hardly ever in anything like allegory. And hardly ever with support of illustrations from chivalry, and with only occasional brief help from the mythology of the ancients. There are wonderful exceptions—the superb *Muiopotmos* above all—but it is still true that in dozens of poems there is no expression except in brief similes of the poetry of the ancient gods or of the world of chivalry, and, of course, no such use of Christian divinities as in Ariosto and Tasso. And until the *Hymns* there is almost no evidence that this poet would ever try an epic or a romance, or a sustained allegory, and only *Daphnaida*, which is rather late and written long after *The Faerie Queene* has been under way, the *Hymns*, and *Muiopotmos* give evidence of ambitiousness. For the great mass of his other writing the single sustaining convention is the uncomplicated pastoral, devoted to the complaint.

One must stress it—the dominant idea is the thoughtful, often cool disappointment with the world. The thought is clear, the language simple, and, surprisingly, often in the plain order of prose. The absence of philosophy is also remarkable: the brief references to poetic inspiration in the *October* eclogue and the cosmological sketch in *Colin Clout's Come Home Again* count for almost nothing. There are a few Christian platitudes, some dramatically Christian sentiment in the poems on Sidney's death—but in these there is really nothing that can be called philosophical. At most, reading them, one understands that one is being given a kind of worldly view, conclusions about the world by a man living in it and holding worldly standards, the honest man observing deceit, failure, and death. In such poems as *Virgils Gnat*, *Muiopotmos*, *Mother Hubberds Tale*, one does not find philosophy but intelligent comment. But however remarkable and extensive Spenser's lucidity, it is often overbalanced by the expression of sorrow for the conditions that cause his trouble. And if *Mother Hubberds Tale* is lucid and disillusioned, other works are generally dominated more by the idea of the complaint than by the idea of clarity.

It is curious, however, how rarely anything like the real thing, the moving personal note, comes through in the elegiac poems, a remarkable series full of the energy of invention and variety of discourse, the metrics brilliant beyond belief. Perhaps the occasions of these poems were too close, and there was no opportunity for the recollection of tranquillity, or perhaps the shepherd's masque was not the proper one for Spenser at such times although it was to serve Milton well enough in *Lycidas*. It seems that for Spenser it kept a kind of fashionableness he had to leave at that. In the remarkable passage in which Sidney is imagined to apologize for his life, perfect in every respect, noble, Christian, the rhetoric faultless, only the anguish is lacking:

O Lord if ought this fraile
And earthly carcasse haue thy seruice sought t'aduaunce,
If my desire haue bene still to relieue th'opprest:
If Iustice to maintaine that valour I haue spent
Which thou me gau'st; or if henceforth I might aduance
Thy name, thy truth, then spare me (Lord) if thou think best;
Forbeare these vnripe yeares. But if thy will be bent,
If that prefixed time be come which thou hast set,
Through pure and feruent faith, I hope now to be plast,
In the' euerlasting blis, which with thy precious blood
Thou purchase didst for vs.

(*The Mourning Muse of Thestylis*, 61–71)

Everything is exactly right, humility, deference, decorum, the rising inflections, the sweep of the voice. But Bolingbroke's lines even with their taint of unctuousness have more blood and faith than this too perfect speech:

Therefore, friends,
As far as to the sepulchre of Christ,
Whose soldier now, under whose blessed cross
We are impressed and engag'd to fight,
Forthwith a power of English shall we levy;
Whose arms were moulded in their mother's womb
To chase these pagans in those holy fields
Over whose acres walk'd those blessed feet
Which fourteen hundred years ago were nail'd
For our advantage on the bitter cross.

(*I Henry IV*. I. i. 18–27)

But before the *Hymns* and the *Epithalamion* the poem in which the passion is strongest, the language plainest, the thought most independent and impious, is *Daphnaida*, another pastoral work, and the one in which the poet as the man, if not of vision, then of solitary regret, is most clearly presented to the reader, the man alone with his complaint, as if Spenser were now taking up Colin's line—

Enough is me to paint out my vnrest—

(*June*, 79)

and giving it the scope of a vision of the world.

The elegy begins in the poet's own narration, himself

> of many most,
> Most miserable man,
>
> (37–8)

but a shepherd, Alcyon, takes over the main part of the poem, telling how the world appears to him who has lost his beloved Daphne to Death.

> She fell away against all course of kinde, (242)
> Hencefoorth I hate whateuer Nature made. (393)
> Let th'earth be barren and bring foorth no flowres. (334)

And Alcyon, deserted, looks forward only to misery:

> My bread shall be the anguish of my mind,
> My drink the teares which fro mine eyes do raine.
>
> (375–6)

He can look upon the rest of his days as nothing other than a useless quest after what can no longer be found in life:

> Her now I seek throughout this earthlie soyle,
> And seeking misse, and missing doe lament.
>
> (167–8)

> For I will walke this wandring pilgrimage
> Throughout the world from one to other end,
> And in affliction waste my better age.
>
> (372–4)

And in one of the most beautiful of all laments—

> And euer as I see the starres to fall,
> And vnder ground to goe, to giue them light
> Which dwell in darknes, I to minde will call,
> How my faire Starre (that shinde on me so bright)
> Fell sodainly, and faded vnder ground.
>
> (477–81)

In this hopelessness one sees the passion of grief express itself in a view of things in which the recognition is finally reached that all is unstable, and man is condemned ever to desire and ever to lack what he desires. The shepherd poet, the man of complaints and visions, has no goal proposed as for a knight, and is lost in a mere wandering pilgrimage. And how different this is from that old complaint in *The Ruines of Time:*

> Ne other comfort in this world can be,
> But hope of heauen, and heart to God inclinde;
> For all the rest must needs be left behinde.
>
> (584–6)

For the imagined singer of *Daphnaida* there is no rest.

The stirring of feeling, in other words, the Spenserian sound, the complaint suddenly expressing power and emotion, begins when the forms he uses take up with the attitude of recollection, and suddenly in that attitude there develops the idea of philosophicalness, of something comprehensive. Poem after poem begins the same way:

> It chaunced me on day beside the shore.
>
> (*The Ruines of Time*)

> One day, whiles that my daylie cares did sleepe.
>
> (*Visions of the Worlds Vanitie*)

> It was the time, when rest soft sliding downe.[1]
>
> (*The Visions of Bellay*)

> Being one day at my window all alone,
> So manie strange things happened me to see,
> As much it grieueth me to thinke thereon.

[1] The inspiration of Du Bellay particularly was most important in the formation of the visionary meditation in Spenser, and the great beauty of Du Bellay's poetry ought to be thought of in this connection and especially for the lucidity of the language. The poem Spenser is here translating goes most beautifully—

> C'estoit alors que le present des dieux
> Plus doulcement s'écoule aux yeux de l'homme,
> Faisant noyer dedans l'oubly du somme
> Tout le soucy du jour laborieux . . .

(*Les Antiquitez de Rome: Songe I*, in *Les Antiquitez de Rome et Les Regrets*, ed. E. Droz, Lille: Librairie Giard, 1947, p. 19.)

At my right hand a Hynde appear'd to mee,
  So faire as mote the greatest God delite;
Two eager dogs did her pursue in chace,
Of which the one was blacke, the other white:
With deadly force so in their cruell race
  They pincht the haunches of that gentle beast,
That at the last, and in short time I spide,
Vnder a Rocke where she alas opprest.
Fell to the ground, and there vntimely dide.
  Cruell death vanquishing so noble beautie,
  Oft makes me wayle so hard a destenie.
(*The Visions of Petrarch*)

Beginning a poem with a story about a dream (or "vision") is, I suppose, an indication of the central point, that the present is unsatisfactory, since the world is neither anxious for the truth nor anxious to provide glory—poetry is not honoured, hypocrisy reigns, love is inconstant. But more than the pastoral form presented in the narrative past, the recollections of the past assembled in the idea of a vision reveal a more absorbing discontent and so give greater room for passion:

One day, whiles that my daylie cares did sleepe,
My spirit, shaking off her earthly prison,
Began to enter into meditation deepe
Of things exceeding reach of common reason;
  Such as this age, in which all good is geason,
And all that humble is and meane debaced,
Hath brought forth in her last declining season,
Griefe of good mindes, to see goodnesse disgraced.
  On which when as my thought was throghly placed,
Vnto my eyes strange showes presented were,
Picturing that, which I in minde embraced,
That yet those sights empassion me full nere.
  Such as they were (faire Ladie) take in worth,
  That when time serues, may bring things better forth.
(*Visions of the Worlds Vanitie*)

And everywhere one may see how much greater scope the "vision" gives, how much chance to vivify the image of the lover complaining than the simple pastoral, just as, in *November* for example, a vision opens a wider world and the lament over the death of Dido becomes a picture of her translation to a happier place:

> Why wayle we then? why weary we the Gods with
> playnts,
> As if some euill were to her betight?
> She raignes a goddesse now emong the saintes,
> That whilome was the saynt of shepheards light:
> And is enstalled nowe in heauens hight.
> I see thee blessed soule, I see,
> Walke in *Elisian* fieldes so free.
> O happy herse,
> Might I once come to thee (O that I might)
> O ioyfull verse.
>
> (173–82)

The scene grows large, something more extensive than a pastoral world, thought and feeling are more deeply engaged, and Spenser has the chance to let himself go. The rejection of the world now develops meaning because the view of things begins to be comprehensive, and in place of comment and the poses of regret, passion can bring life to the figures and sentiments because reason and philosophy are beginning to support it.

From the complaint, nostalgia, "visions," there comes the beginning of what may always be most important for poetry, praise. This is sometimes in an invocation or an incantation, and sometimes with an overwhelming beauty in the simple naming and ordering of things,

> We now haue playde (*Augustus*) wantonly,
> Tuning our song vnto a tender Muse,
> And like a cobweb weauing slenderly,
> Haue onely playde.
>
> (*Virgils Gnat*, 1–4)

And mightily:

Most glorious Lord of lyfe, that on this day,
  Didst make thy triumph ouer death and sin:
  and hauing harrowd hell, didst bring away
  captiuity thence captiue vs to win:
This ioyous day, deare Lord, with ioy begin,
  and grant that we for whom thou diddest dye
  being with thy deare blood clene washt from sin,
  may liue for euer in felicity.
And that thy loue we weighing worthily,
  may likewise loue thee for the same againe:
  and for thy sake that all lyke deare didst buy,
  with loue may one another entertayne.
So let vs loue, deare loue, lyke as we ought,
  loue is the lesson which the Lord vs taught.

(*Sonnet* LXVIII)

The *Hymns* became the first, direct, full utterance, Spenser writing with all his power, and all that there had been in the other poems of the lyrical impulse, of thought about love and perfection and sadness, now as it were came to know itself. Here, more accented than in *The Shepheardes Calender*, or the *Visions*, or anywhere, there is before us the image of the single figure, but not merely in the posture of complaint or as a man dreaming, but the image above all else of a man praising, even as if he were in the presence of the gods, and in language of such directness and strength there is hardly anything to equal it except the Biblical force:

Great god of might, that reignest in the mynd,
And all the bodie to thy hest doest frame,
Victor of gods, subduer of mankynd,
That doest the Lions and fell Tigers tame,
Making their cruell rage thy scornefull game.
And in their roring taking great delight;
Who can expresse the glorie of thy might?

(*Hymne of Love*, 43–9)

Again and again the tremendous invocations:

> Loue, that long since hast to thy mighty powre,
> Perforce subdude my poore captiued hart.
>
> (*Hymne of Love*, 1–2)

> Thereto do thou great Goddesse, queene of Beauty,
> Mother of loue, and of all worlds delight,
> Without whose souerayne grace and kindly dewty.
> Nothing on earth seemes fayre to fleshly sight,
> Doe thou vouchsafe with thy loue-kindling light,
> T'illuminate my dim and dulled eyne,
> And beautifie this sacred hymne of thyne.
>
> (*Hymne of Beautie*, 15–21)

> Loue, lift me vp vpon thy golden wings,
> From this base world vnto thy heauens hight,
> Where I may see those admirable things,
> Which there thou workest by thy soueraine might,
> Farre aboue feeble reach of earthly sight.
>
> (*Hymne of Heavenly Love*, 1–5)

The great marriage songs are also hymns, and there, too, invocation has its part, lending its tone to the holy solemnities:

> Ye learned sisters which haue oftentimes
> Beene to me ayding, others to adorne:
> Whom ye thought worthy of your gracefull rymes,
> That euen the greatest did not greatly scorne
> To heare theyr names sung in your simple layes,
> But ioyed in theyr prayse. (*Epithalamion*, 1–6)

Yet more than from invocation the poetry in these two songs gets its chief beauty from the simple naming of things as they are, naming for all the charm of names:

> Calme was the day, and through the trembling ayre,
> Sweete breathing *Zephyrus* did softly play
> A gentle spirit, that lightly did delay
> Hot *Titans* beames, which then did glyster fayre.
>
> (*Prothalamion*, 1–4)

And even as such description leads into the preparation for the recital of a vision, the simplicity of the description carries the chief power.

> When I whom sullein care,
> Through discontent of my long fruitlesse stay
> In Princes Court, and expectation vayne
> Of idle hopes, which still doe fly away,
> Like empty shaddowes, did aflict my brayne,
> Walkt forth to ease my payne
> Along the shoare of siluer streaming *Themmes*,
> Whose rutty Bancke, the which his Riuer hemmes,
> Was paynted all with variable flowers,
> And all the meades adornd with daintie gemmes,
> Fit to decke maydens bowres,
> And crowne their Paramours,
> Against the Brydale day, which is not long:
>   Sweete *Themmes* runne softly, till I end my Song.
>
> There, in a meadow, by the Riuers side,
> A Flocke of *Nymphes* I chaunced to espy . . . .
>
> (5–20)

The sense of truthfulness is everywhere, and what is sometimes taken for philosophy often is not that. What might be a doctrine is also something more than a doctrine—

> For all that faire is, is by nature good—
>
> (*Hymne of Beautie*, 139)

it is something felt to be more true than any explanation. And questions that sometimes imply answers of a philosophical kind are also suggestions of mere experience, truths endured, facts, one might say, of such a kind recorded without any dreaming of philosophy by Sappho and Catullus:

> Hath white and red in it such wondrous powre,
> That it can pierce through th'eyes vnto the hart,
> And therein stirre such rage and restlesse stowre,
> As nought but death can stint his dolours smart?

Or can proportion of the outward part,
Moue such affection in the inward mynd,
That it can rob both sense and reason blynd?

(*Hymne of Beautie*, 71–7)

Something of the same simplicity of statement is true of what can be taken as more complex ideas:

But they which loue indeede, looke otherwise,
With pure regard and spotlesse true intent,
Drawing out of the obiect of their eyes,
A more refyned forme, which they present
Vnto their mind, voide of all blemishment;
Which it reducing to her first perfection,
Beholdeth free from fleshes frayle infection.

And then conforming it vnto the light,
Which in it selfe it hath remaining still
Of that first Sunne, yet sparckling in his sight,
Thereof he fashions in his higher skill,
An heauenlie beautie to his fancies will,
And it embracing in his mind entyre,
The mirrour of his owne thought doth admyre,

(*Hymne of Beautie*, 211–24)

There are, of course, interpretations here in all the derivations of Platonic psychology, but there is primarily described in such lines the fact, the common truth of the way love works:

The gnawing enuie, the hart-fretting feare,
The vaine surmizes, the distrustfull showes,
The false reports that flying tales doe beare,
The doubts, the daungers, the delayes, the woes,
The fayned friends, the vnassured foes,
With thousands more then any tongue can tell,
Doe make a louers life a wretches hell.

(*Hymne of Love*, 259–65)

For the point to all these hymns is in their truth, as simple as may be statements to acknowledge and praise the force of love. And the hymns say in all their glorious power what was first in those gentle statements in the pastorals and the other shorter poems, that for Spenser love is always at the heart of life, and he must grow to the fullest celebration of it in himself. This will be much of the substance of *The Faerie Queene*, too, except that there he must also speak of justice. But in the *Hymns*, in the apostrophe to Love, it is he following the god in the way Una follows the Red Crosse Knight:

> Thou art his god, thou art his mightie guyde,
> Thou being blind, letst him not see his feares,
> But carriest him to that which he hath eyde,
> Through seas, through flames, through thousand swords
> and speares:
> Ne ought so strong that may his force withstand,
> With which thou armest his resistlesse hand.
>
> (*Hymne of Love*, 225–30)

Here again there is the image of the single figure led through the world, its dangers, its hostility, and the poet is really speaking to himself, thinking of himself in this strange and terrible world, only now the note of plainness and humility is transformed into power and glory.

And finally, there is this, that all the hymns are to be understood as a singing to himself—

> Ah whither, Loue, wilt thou now carrie mee?
>
> (*Hymne of Beautie*, 1)

> O blessed well of loue, O floure of grace,
> O glorious Morning starre, O lampe of light,
> Most liuely image of thy fathers face,
> Eternall King of glorie, Lord of might,
> Meeke lambe of God before all worlds behight,
> How can we thee requite for all this good?
> Or what can prize that thy most precious blood?
>
> Yet nought thou ask'st in lieu of all this loue,
> But loue of vs for guerdon of thy paine.
> Ay me; what can vs lesse then that behoue?

Had he required life of vs againe,
Had it beene wrong to ask his owne with gaine?
He gaue vs life, he it restored lost;
Then life were least, that vs so litle cost.

(*Hymne of Heavenly Love*, 169–82)

However much to be known as hymns, these addresses to Love and the Muses and Christ are not meant to be delivered to those persons, but to himself, and such poems in the end are a singing to himself, and the tone of the individual in meditation, measured and enthusiastic, is the final determinant of the poem's form and strength. As such inward conversation begins—

Rapt with the rage of mine own rauisht thought,
Through contemplation of those goodly sights,
And glorious images in heauen wrought,
Whose wondrous beauty breathing sweet delights,
Do kindle loue in high conceipted sprights:
I faine to tell the things that I behold,
But feele my wits to faile, and tongue to fold.—

(*Hymne of Heavenly Beautie*, 1–7)

there then starts an invocation, the simple extension of his appraisal of himself:

Vouchsafe then, O thou most almightie Spright,
From whom all guifts of wit and knowledge flow,
To shed into my breast some sparkling light
Of thine eternall Truth, that I may show
Some little beames to mortall eyes below,
Of that immortall beautie, there with thee,
Which in my weake distraughted mynd I see.

(8–14)

In the first hymn there is the abiding truth,

For loue is Lord of truth and loialtie,

(*Hymne of Love*, 176)

and what ravages him, the love of woman or of beauty, is also always the love of holiness, and the initial terms are the same to talk about the love of Christ:

> O huge and most vnspeakeable impression
> Of loues deepe wound, that pierst the piteous hart
> Of that deare Lord with so entyre affection,
> And sharply launching euery inner part,
> Dolours of death into his soule did dart;
> Doing him die, that neuer it deserued,
> To free his foes, that from his heast had swerued.[1]
>
> (*Hymne of Heavenly Love*, 155–61)

And there, again, the final emphasis is on the single figure, the individual, praying:

> Ah then my hungry soule, which long hast fed
> On idle fancies of thy foolish thought,
> And with false beauties flattring bait misled,
> Hast after vaine deceiptfull shadowes sought,
> Which all are fled, and now haue left thee nought,
> But late repentance through thy follies prief;
> Ah ceasse to gaze on matter of thy grief.
>
> And looke at last vp to that soueraine light,
> From whose pure beams al perfect beauty springs,
> That kindleth loue in euery godly spright,
> Euen the loue of God, which loathing brings
> Of this vile world, and these gay seeming things;
> With whose sweete pleasures being so possest,
> Thy straying thoughts henceforth for euer rest.
>
> (*Hymne of Heavenly Beautie*, 288–301)

[1] The Anacreontic figure of the heart wounded by love and the Christian figure of speech are intermixed in the conception of the love that enthralls Arthur. Una once asked him,

> Ah curteous knight (quoth she) what secret wound
> Could euer find, to grieue the gentlest hart on ground?
>
> (I. ix. 7)

The Romantic Scene

I

If there is in Spenser's poetry from the earliest time a concentration on the singlefigure, there always remains, in *The Faerie Queene* as in *The Shepheardes Calender* and in the *Hymnes*, the question of what it is, what understanding or what faith, can subdue the variety of things to the quester's need; what in the pattern of things gives reason to believe that that questing or beseeching figure can derive strength and support from the world, and so go on to his perfection;[1] what it is that will show that he can

[1] The Proem to the sixth book of *The Faerie Queene* expresses something of the feeling of the narrator towards the scene of his knights' adventures, and it raises this very question.

> The waies, through which my weary steps I guyde,
> In this delightfull land of Faery,
> Are so exceeding spacious and wyde,
> And sprinckled with such sweet variety,
> Of all that pleasant is to eare or eye,
> That I nigh rauisht with rare thoughts delight,
> My tedious trauell doe forget thereby;
> And when I gin to feele decay of might,
> It strength to me supplies, and chears my dulled spright.
>
> Such secret comfort, and such heauenly pleasures,
> Ye sacred imps, that on *Parnasso* dwell,
> And there the keeping haue of learnings threasures,
> Which doe all worldy riches farre excell,
> Into the mindes of mortall men doe well,
> And goodly fury into them infuse;
> Guyde ye my footing, and conduct me well
> In these strange waies, where neuer foote did vse,
> Ne none can find, but who was taught them by the Muse.
>
> Reuele to me the sacred noursery
> Of vertue, which with you doth there remaine,
> Where it in siluer bowre does hidden ly
> From view of men, and wicked worlds disdaine.

overcome the terror of mutability, the trouble that was expressed at the beginning in the *Ruines of Time* as well as in those last cantos:

> All things doo change that vnder heauen abide,
> And after death all friendship doth decaie.
> Therefore what euer man bearst worldlie sway,
> Liuing, on God, and on thy selfe relie;
> For when thou diest, all shall with thee die.
>
> (*Ruines of Time*, 206–10)

At the very beginning too, there was the awful observation of Thenot's:

> All that is lent to loue, wyll be lost.
>
> (*Februarie*, 70)

In *The Shepheardes Calender* there are a few clearly emphasized themes, the pain of a love that is not returned, the power of change and death over life, the tarnishing even of religion by ambition, and the contempt of poetry. It is the abuses that are emphasized although one understands how much Spenser means to praise what was always to have honour, love, the faithfully religious, and poetry. Yet *The Shepheardes Calender* offers no scheme in which we see how love and religion and poetry work together for faith and constancy, even in the affairs of men, to say nothing of the universe. The beliefs and regrets are manifest, but the thought is not developed. The questions there and elsewhere are the elementary, terrible ones, and if in the early poems the answers are not systematic, the single affirmation that is repeated again and again is the idea of the power and excellence of love.

In so many ways this will be the principle to guide the knights of *The Faerie Queene*, and although for all its promise of stability it gives itself to the things it seeks to praise and eternize, it too is faced with inevitable death:

> They all are gone, and all with them is gone,
> Ne ought to me remaines, but to lament
> My long decay, which no man els doth mone,
> And mourne my fall with dolefull dreriment.
>
> (*Ruines of Time*, 155–8)

But if the nature of love is thus unfortunate, to contribute to the change it means to destroy, it is nevertheless Spenser's all but everlasting hope of providing an explanation for things, and the idea of the constancy of love will make it possible for him to look towards some completeness finally, in his imagination at least and perhaps in religion.

In such an effort, from such a necessity Spenser's conception as he works it out in his poetry must be his own, it must provide a view of love which will give meaning to such a complex world as the scene a romance demands. It will be, of course, an improvement over Ariosto, where love leads in the end to madness. It will need to go so far that it will show the way to justice, perhaps it will be known as the creator of justice.

The poem must show that order and constancy depend upon the love of the Creator and the love of justice and the love of truth, in oneself and in society and in the universe, as it is with the love that moves Arthur, Britomart, Amoret, Calidore. But in the Faerie Land that is their world and in this respect the world of humans, too, the demands of love are for missions and quests on behalf of justice, and for fulfilments yet to be known that belong to the plans of Providence. Thus it is that the reader of *The Faerie Queene* is led into an understanding of the power of love as he learns to know the nature of the world in which he sees the wanderings of these innumerable persons with their single aims.[1]

The purpose of *The Faerie Queene* is to tell of knights and ladies, their deeds and their loves, and the form of the story is initially *le roman educatif*, the romance of a knight whose trials fit him for a final, major success. Ultimately the completed work will tell us of the greatest victory of the greatest Christian knight, overcoming unnamed enemies and gaining the hand of the Queen.

The achievements of a few of the knights of the poem partly

[1] Edwin Greenlaw has been one of the few writers on Spenser who has recognized that the situations of romance in themselves are often significant, what he called symbolic, and thus, as distinct from allegory, carry quite as evidently a burden of meaning and instruction. (Review of Herbert E. Cory's *Edmund Spenser*, in *Modern Language Notes*, xxxv [1920], 165–75.)

belong to Arthur, with his timely aid, but his and their accomplishments alike depend on the same virtues. Their successes are those of courage and temperance and justice and faith, but their ends are attained only through God's will and grace—all knightly achievement is possible only through that. It is the Red Crosse Knight who says what no other could say differently:

> His be the praise, that this atchieu'ment wrought,
> Who made my hand the organ of his might;
> More then goodwill to me attribute nought:
> For all I did, I did but as I ought.
>
> (II. i. 33)

The knights oppose force and malice, in a field of action where evil, without the intervention of grace, would often be triumphant. Faerie Land is indeed a place where there is all but unlimited evil, and where it is free to take every conceivable form. And it is a place where the side of virtue, however supported by grace, is represented only by mortals. Except in the Pastorella episode and the story of Chrysogone and her twins, there are no good divinities to take part in the story, and even then they are no part of the main adventures. And nowhere in the poem is there any visit to the islands of the moon as in the *Orlando Furioso*, and no scene in Heaven where God holds court, as in the *Gerusalemme Liberata*. God Himself makes Himself known only through His servants and those who are the recipients of grace. If the underworld is visited it is only by spirits, and however heavenly any pastoral scene might be there are no glimpses either of an earthly paradise.

What is chiefly important for the story is that evil shall take every imaginable form, that the value of grace may be known by its power over all the enemies of virtue, just as the power of each knight is known by the strength of each dragon and sorcerer and witch that tests him. Every imaginable form, the beautiful, the disgusting, the unintelligible, even the insignificant, the scene must be crowded, there must be a vast multitude of evil things and creatures, growing, spreading everywhere. The crowd and the vast variety of evil must be like a forest, springing up everywhere and ever denser and denser. As for Una and St. George at the beginning of their adventures:

> When weening to returne, whence they did stray,
> They cannot finde that path, which first was showne,
> But wander too and fro in wayes vnknowne,
> Furthest from end then, when they neerest weene,
> That makes them doubt, their wits be not their owne. . . .
>
> At last resoluing forward still to fare,
> Till that some end they finde or in or out,
> That path they take, that beaten seemd most bare,
> And like to lead the labyrinth about;
> Which when by tract they hunted had throughout,
> At length it brought them to a hollow caue,
> Amid the thickest woods.
>
> (I. i. 10, 11)

Such as it is, in its variety and confusion, the Faerie Land of the poem is a place for humans and for their human Queen—at least for individuals more like humans than any other variety of creature. They are called Faeries and Elves. The qualification brings with it nothing of the supernatural, and there remains only the endowment belonging to them as Christians, possessing holy purposes. These individuals, whose lives are governed by chivalry, exist in a world where the evils they confront are always absolute—they have no enemies of good and evil mixed, only the wholly evil whose outward appearance is sometimes deceptive. To this wholeness in the character of evil the good oppose the character of simplicity, for they are deprived of the complexity and depth that must be brought to bear in living in the ordinary world.

With this simplicity goes the other quality of greatest importance in the subjects of Gloriana, the disposition for love and the quality of soul that creates that disposition.

It takes various forms, the love of Christ, of God, of country, of justice, of truth, and most frequently and perhaps genially the love of humans for each other, and especially romantic love.

But here again, variety, the various loves, and the missions of justice and patriotism and courtship that belong with them add to the other plenitude, the other crowding of life, to mix with the luxuriant, the inexhaustible, the ingenious variety of evil. As if to say that the richness of evil is matched by the inexhaustible richness of love.

Thus it is, I think, that the mere variety of the scene comes to take precedence in the definition of Faerie Land over any philosophic or allegorical intention. This country is not conceived as Dante's and Bunyan's scenes, as one in which so many details have meaning for philosophy or religion, in which perhaps each detail has its part in a scheme understood by the intellect and by religion. Here there is much that is uninterpretable, that exists merely for the interest of itself as an object in the world, beautiful, sometimes, as Arthur's helmet, but interesting merely as something in itself and in its beauty or ugliness, and not for its significance, should any be attached to it:

> His haughtie helmet, horrid all with gold,
> Both glorious brightnesse, and great terrour bred;
> For all the crest a Dragon did enfold
> With greedie pawes, and ouer all did spred
> His golden wings: his dreadfull hideous hed
> Close couched on the beuer, seem'd to throw
> From flaming mouth bright sparkles fierie red,
> That suddeine horror to faint harts did show;
> And scaly tayle was stretcht adowne his backe full low.
>
> (*F. Q.* I. vii. 31)

Thousands of details of no interpretable meaning, even in actions patently in part allegorical, and so that Faerie Land may be known first of all for its divine variety. The details that are intelligible in a special way—self-consuming Error and the like—are merely something else in the variety. To the degree that they represent some half-philosophic understanding of the nature of Faerie Land and so become parts of a scheme of things, they will be understood to be parts of the world which schemes against the perfection of love, either through casual malice or helped by some imperfection in the lover, as through some fault in the knight's devotion to truth or justice or to his mistress. Evil will also be the unintelligible mistakenly loved. There will also be times when love will be philosophically conceived, and at other times it will be justified only by its existence. It is such at once natural and miraculous affirmations that restrict the philosophy of the poem so that Faerie Land is not like the wood of *Comus*, the world seen by a Platonist. It will sometimes be that, but it will also be the world of Una and the Lion, of Una and the Savage Nation, of Pastorella and the Graces—beauty and wonder free from philosophical attention, imagined in the mere simplicity of love and trust and wonder.

II

It is easy to see how Spenser goes about to define the scene of the figures of his imagination for it is a simple method consistently followed. The manner of the beginning of the poem is kept to the end, and the terms of the arbitrary limiting of the fantastic world are immediately clear.

The book begins by saying a knight is riding somewhere, and neither he nor the destination is named:

> A Gentle Knight was pricking on the plaine,
> Y cladd in mightie armes and siluer shielde,
> Wherein old dints of deepe woundes did remaine,
> The cruell markes of many' a bloudy fielde;
> Yet armes till that time did he neuer wield.

He rides a restive horse, and there is someone with him:

> A louelie Ladie rode him faire beside,
> Vpon a lowly Asse more white then snow.
>
> (I. i. 4)

She is followed, rather oddly, by a lamb, and at a greater distance—

> Behind her farre away a Dwarfe did lag,
> That lasie seemd in being euer last.
>
> (I. i. 6)

Each figure is thus mentioned singly, there are a few words to describe the dress of each and the dominant colours chiefly, somewhat more to signify the states of mind of these travellers, and nothing to describe the setting. It is merely a "plaine."

There is no conversation among the three, and no comment by the teller on their destination. Three personages are baldly presented to us so that we begin to wonder about their identity and their nature, and our curiosity grows as the scene shifts from strangeness to strangeness.

First, it gets dark:

Thus as they past,
The day with cloudes was suddeine ouercast,
And angry *Ioue* an hideous storme of raine
Did poure into his Lemans lap so fast,
That euery wight to shrowd it did constrain,
And this faire couple eke to shroud themselues were fain.
(I. i. 6)

When they enter the wood for shelter the kinds of trees there are named—

The sayling Pine, the Cedar proud and tall—
(I. i. 8)

and so on, and in their midst the knight and lady move in as alien a world as the empty plain, beautiful and alien, meaning no more to them, nor will any scene to any character in the poem, than a place of shelter or rest or dalliance, a place to admire or a place to cross. The scene, the setting, the forest, the world is meaningless, a mere condition for existence, for traversing, for enduring, for leaving, a thing of trial or convenience, but with no link to the harmony of things, to the humans in it no part of some great chain of being as in the *Timaeus* where one spirit breathes through the world's body and in the creatures on the earth. The scene, the universe, is what circumscribes men and women, nothing more; it offers them no guidance, and it echoes to no need. It is merely a plain or a wandering wood or *Errours den*, and any transformation it may endure in order to serve a human purpose is only in the mind. The Red Crosse Knight too vainly claims

> Vertue giues her selfe light, through darkenesse for to wade.
> (I. i. 12)

But nature itself does not conspire, as in *Comus*, to send sun or moon through the clouds to guide the lost.

The scene and everything indeed outside the mind and heart is regarded by Spenser as something with no rights of its own, no life whose definition he must treat with awe. It is a world recognizably like the real one, the earth green, trees growing into the clouds, streams running to the sea, but except for such elemental similarities it is what he wants to make of it, changed and charged according to the way at any moment nature may seem to serve or hinder the interests of love and justice and truth. The monster *Errour*, half-woman half-serpent, has black blood; agreeably to the various allegorical suggestions we take this to signify ink, one of the means of propagating lies. But the first point is that this monster's blood is not like any other's, it is black. The blood, the wandering wood, the cave, the waterfall near where Morpheus is sleeping—they are as they are, dense or dark or in the midst of music as it pleases Spenser to make them, in order to serve his intellectual designs, to make the story seem remarkable, and sometimes to illustrate incidentally, even wantonly, a point about how men may go wrong or right. Even the richest scene bears the essential characters of *la Forêt gaste*. To be in such a universe means above all that

> It is the mynd, that maketh good or ill,
> (VI. ix. 30)

and this is more consistently a comment on the unintelligibility of Faerie Land than the expression of a Platonic commitment.

And thus for all the variety of the scene and the wealth of fancy, nature and all physical things exist in the poem as given, mysterious facts, necessary in their usual meaninglessness as a scene for a poet writing about knights and ladies whose purposes are those of Christians. The single principle to govern the setting of all the poem is a principle of art: the subservience of nature to the wilful distortions of the imagination, in the contempt of verisimilitude and in the pleasure of observing how the mind creates the grotesque and beautiful. The reader is left to think about what all this means to man in the ordinary world, who also for so much of the time is left alone with his mind.[1]

To consider the character of Faerie Land as an arbitrarily conceived setting, and thus as a place differently conceived than the world of the Platonic philosophers is important in order that we may not demand of the poem a unity in allegorical conception it need not have. Reality, one recognizes, to a Platonist and certain others, is itself allegorical, but for all Spenser's Platonism so much cannot be said of the reality, the world in which the characters of *The Faerie Queene* live. The variety and confusion of their world has no single key, no order in any philosophical direction the poet takes from time to time, and it is for all the fantastic part a world more like the chaos of common sense than anything else. But the fantastic part has of course itself a more important value to the poem, not only in the poem's structure, but in the way it helps

[1] Greenlaw spoke of the arbitrary combination of the romance and folklore worlds in *The Faerie Queene* together with the presentation of contemporary historical matter, and then he considered the way in which the significance of the "vision" provides the basis for the union of these worlds. ("Spenser's Fairy Mythology," *Studies in Philology*, XV [1918], 107, 116.) I believe this is a fair way of stating Spenser's approach, and as I understand Greenlaw's meaning it is one the present study supports up to the point where historical allegory is certifiable. As with the *Divine Comedy* the historical references seem to me to be assimilated within the romantic conception, to offer nothing foreign to the poem and its movement even when one needs to bring information to bear not alluded to in the words of the poem. In *The Faerie Queene* as in the *Divine Comedy* it is not so much the historical allegory that distracts us as the commentary that would force us too violently to read the lines and their references in the context of history alone.

W. L. Renwick's discussion of the integration of allegorical and æsthetic values is a useful beginning towards stating the terms of the problem (*Edmund Spenser*, London, 1925, pp. 142–50).

define the values the poem manifests through the emphasis it receives from the attitude of the narrator.

For this imaginative scene deserves to be thought of as the scene of a dream or a vision, although there are no such statements as Dante gives us to say so. And we can see something of its peculiar character by contrasting it with Spenser's usual pastoral world. In *The Shepheardes Calender* the progression of the months carries with it an analogy to the course of life, and in the Argument to *December* the analogy is plainly stated:

> This Æglogue (euen as the first beganne) is ended with a complaynte of Colin to God Pan. Wherein as weary of his former wayes, he proportioneth his life to the foure seasons of the yeare, comparing hys youthe to the spring time, when he was fresh and free from loues follye. His manhoode to the sommer which he sayth, was consumed with greate heate and excessiue drouth caused throughe a Comet or blasing starre, by which hee meaneth loue, which passion is comenly compared to such flames and immoderate heate. His riper years hee resembleth to an vnseasonable harueste wherein the fruites fall ere they be rype. His latter age to winters chyll and frostie season, now drawing neare to his last ende.

There is more to *The Shepheardes Calender* than this, for life has meant not merely the failure of Colin's love, and there have been other trials and misfortunes, the loss of sheep, the loss of friends, journeys away from the country to inhospitable places, various pains apart from death, and corruption in the church. And the poem has fallen short of the most severe distress because as a pastoral it has preserved one of the conditions of that form, that it should present a life where the greatest evils are not often known (though there is the death of Tityrus), where the state of innocence is not yet (perhaps) lost, in short where something remains of the Earthly Paradise and in which grief and pain are not often as desperate as Colin's premonitions:

> Tell me good Hobbinoll, what garres thee greete?
> What? hath some Wolfe thy tender Lambes ytorne?
> Or is thy Bagpipe broke, that soundes so sweete?
> Or art thou of thy loued lasse forlorne?
>
> (*Aprill*, 1–4)

And if not everywhere in *The Shepheardes Calender* there is paradise, there is something very much like it in a certain part, or was once:

Then if by me thou list aduised be,
Forsake the soyle, that so doth the bewitch:
Leaue me those hilles, where harbrough nis to see,
Nor holybush, nor brere, nor winding witche:
And to the dales resort, where shepheards ritch,
And fruictfull flocks bene euery where to see.
Here no night Rauens lodge more black then pitche,
Nor eluish ghosts, nor gastly owles doe flee.

But frendly Faeries, met with many Graces,
And lightfote Nymphes can chace the lingring night,
With Heydeguyes, and trimly trodden traces,
Whilst systers nyne, which dwell on *Parnasse* hight,
Doe make them musick, for their more delight:
And *Pan* himselfe to kisse their christall faces,
Will pype and daunce, when *Phœbe* shineth bright:
Such pierlesse pleasures haue we in these places.

(*June*, 17–32)

To turn from poetry with a setting in the golden world to *The Faerie Queene* is to turn to poetry where the setting is chiefly determined by romantic tradition, and in a peculiar way by the tradition of vision writing. And here the poet, as someone presented to the reader in a certain role, has peculiar importance. In the preliminary lines to *The Faerie Queene* Spenser, introducing himself as

the man, whose Muse whilome did maske,
As time her taught, in lowly Shepheards weeds,

goes on to call upon the chief of Muses to support him in his grand work, and on Elizabeth.

Shed thy faire beames into my feeble eyne,
And raise my thoughts too humble and too vile,
To thinke of that true glorious type of thine,
The argument of mine afflicted stile.

As the first story begins, the new character he is assuming becomes clearer, and we see this first in the limitations he imposes upon his scene, that "I" who will stay with us to the end as book follows book. The poet who earlier in one or another shepherd's mask sang his own complaints, is here in another mask, contriving another expression in order to give his own thoughts and desires and conclusions their fullest strength. He begins the Book of Justice by a description of the Golden Age, and then he tells how Arthegall was brought up by Astraea in the days of innocence, and the virtue he continues to serve in the corrupted world he learned about them.

Something of the age of innocence remains, too, in all the stories of love, and enough to make the wonderful Pastorella story simply harmonious with the chivalric world of the imagination. And if pastorals look towards some period of the world's history before man was corrupted and if they try to recall some memory of that state, the world of *The Faerie Queene* might be thought of, from one view, as an age not too long after the state of innocence, where the memory of it is strong enough to inspire the passions for its return, and the return of Justice and courtesy and the rest. As it is in *Don Quixote:*

> "Sancho, my friend, you must know that, by the will of Heaven, I was born in this iron age of ours to revive the age of gold or, as it is generally called, the golden age. It is for me that are reserved perils, mighty feats, and valorous exploits. It is I, I say once more, who must revive the order of the Round Table, the Twelve Peers of France, and the Nine Worthies, and consign to oblivion the Platirs, Tablantes, Olivantes and Tirantes, the Knights of the Sun and the Belianises, and all that herd of famous knights errant of olden times, by performing in this age in which I live such prodigies, such wonders, and such feats of arms as to eclipse the most famous deeds they ever performed."[1]

Put another way, the characters of the poem are most of them (to begin with) more anxious for a return of the earthly paradise than for the return of Astraea, or for their own translation to the

[1] *The Adventures of Don Quixote*, tr. J. M. Cohen, Middlesex: Penguin Books, 1950, Part I, ch. xx, p. 149.

skies. And the conditions of this world, the romantic scene, differently than the pastoral, are limited more strictly by the vision of perfected love and the ways to it, they are more closely bound to the lyric writer's purposes, and to the image of the poet, entranced, singing to himself, about himself, alone in the world, and what he sings is a vision:

> Rapt with the rage of mine owne rauisht thought . . .
> I faine to tell the things that I behold.
> (*Hymne of Heavenly Beautie*, 1, 6)

> Helpe then, O holy Virgin chiefe of nine,
> Thy weaker Nouice to performe thy will,
> Lay forth out of thine euerlasting scryne
> The antique rolles, which there lye hidden still.
> (Proem to *F. Q.* ii)

> A Gentle Knight was pricking on the plaine—

It sounds at first as if this might be the ordinary world, where armour is dented, a horse rages, there is a plain to cross. The story goes back far in time, we begin to think, when we know that the knight bears a cross, and this reminder in itself brings something with it of the elusiveness of the past; but soon we learn that there is more to it than this, that this is not the world we know, not even in history, and it is something that requires the name of Faerie Land.

What this means first is that the people in it are always greater, better or worse, than those of the everyday world. It means, too, that there are many unusual, fantastic things and events, that would not be known in the contemporary world—dragons, people turned into trees, a maiden followed by a lamb; some things that are possible, some not, and if one might generalize it would be to say that the quality necessary to anything in Faerie Land is that the features that might bear resemblance to ordinary ones are here exaggerated to extremes. We know fierce serpents, the dragon is the fiercest; we may know the blindness of some passions, but that of those turned into trees is still greater; the gentleness of Una is such that even the beasts follow her trustingly. And if everything must bear the mark of some extreme of beauty or ugliness or good or evil or strength or weakness, nothing must seem ordinary.

So much one might say of Heaven and Hell, yet there must be something else here to distinguish the romantic scene, and perhaps the terms for that are grotesque and picturesque, the extreme for its own sake, for its own interest to the imagination, to satisfy the desire for thinking about things recognizably related to things in the real world, but endowed with the all but irresponsible magnifying of the fantastic imagination. The pleasures and pains are heightened, and the commonplace, the small lies are absent.

The right for such exclusions is apparently determined by the terms of the relationship between the fantastic and the real, by the terms of the relationship between an errant knight on a most adventurous mission and those of any man riding a horse through a wood; between Una as someone whose face casts a light in darkness and a young girl whose parents have been captured by a bandit. The terms of the relationship, which keep preserving the necessary vestiges of verisimilitude to the ordinary world, are that the imagination's faculty to intensify and to magnify is fundamentally a faculty that is not unfaithful to reality and is indeed an intelligible translation of reality—intelligible because it is moved solely by the desire to meet every eventuality, and especially the extreme, the desire to confront the greatest and the worst, to live at the highest pitch, to play for the highest stakes—all in order to demonstrate that the petty world is the great world if one meets it greatly, giving the imagination its chance to show the relationship between reality and greatness. Even as for Don Quixote:

"The tables will be removed, and suddenly there will enter through the hall door an ugly little dwarf with a beautiful lady following behind him, escorted by two giants, to introduce a certain adventure, so contrived by a most ancient sage that the knight who brings it to a successful conclusion shall be accounted the best in the world."[1]

[1] *The Adventures of Don Quixote*, Part I, ch. xxi, p. 166.

The scene of such a romance as *The Faerie Queene* is thus, to begin with, imaginative and fantastic, in order to satisfy the desire to live greatly where it is immediately possible to, in the imagination. It is different from Olympus or Heaven, where life is lived in splendour, in that it proposes a way of living, it suggests a possibility—whereas those others describe what is for faith a fact.

There is thus an essential condition that the world of the poem shall always be considered to be a world apart from the real one, that our concerns are therefore to be aroused differently than for the real one, that we shall be led only into the world of the imagination for the sake of the reality of the imagination, but not for the sake of the world it describes. There is the essential condition of falseness, for its beauty, its strangeness, and for the ordering of matters in such a way that the imagination's own meanings may be understood, and that we may supply the translation, the references it may have for the real world. These may be of the fewest, and ordinarily those fewest would be those to be discovered in the definition of the desire to create a world of the extravagant; in the motive of the desire, to avoid meanness; the search for meaning in the greatest and most intensely conceived matters. This is partly the desire for the heroic, and partly the desire of the pure in heart, partly the dream of holiness. And the desire is also in part the desire to give oneself up only to the meaning in the imagination, and to no other world. Such a desire makes the very scene a way of praising all that is wonderful.

Tasso worked gradually towards his beautiful definition of an epic (or romantic) poem as "an imitation of illustrious actions, complete and great, told in most noble verse, and made with this purpose, to move men's minds with wonder, and thus to their profit."[1] He needed to be particularly careful in his valuing of wonder since he believed, following Aristotle, that he could not admit that the imitation that was the substance of poetry could be

[1] "Diremo dunque che il poema eroico sia imitazione d'azione illustre, grande e perfetta, fatta, narrando con altissimo verso, a fine di muover gli animi con la maraviglia, e di giovare in questa guisa." (*Discorsi del Poema Eroica*, in *Prose*, ed Francesco Flora, Milan, 1935, p. 334. Flora's edition of this work follows the Milan critical edition of 1824.)

of things divine as well as human—it must be restricted to the human. If there were gods in the poem, it could be as with Homer an imitation of gods only in those qualities they share with humans.[1] He had also to account for the use of hybrids, men with features of beasts such as Cinocefalo and Anubis, as primarily human imitations,[2] and I suppose beings like Spenser's fairies and elves correspond to these. He had also to reject, but this time on Platonic grounds, as second-hand imitation, the idea of some critics that fables and indeed all narrative poetry begin in dreams and have dreams as their end:

> If all actions can be imitated, since there are many kinds of action there will be many kinds of poems; and because in this equivocal classification, as Simplicius says in his Sermons, the first kind is contemplation, which is an action of the intellect, contemplation also can be imitated by the poet. As it seems to some persons, Dante's poem has contemplation for its subject because his going to Hell and Purgatory signifies nothing other than the speculations of his mind. Others would have it that the subject of imitation is a dream, as that of Petrarch's *Triumphs* and Boccaccio's *Amorous Vision*. But those who hold this opinion do so in the face of greater opposition, for according to Plato such a poet would not be a proper imitator, since the first degree of truth is the idea, the second the natural form and the thing itself, and the third its imitation or image. But an imitator who makes a likeness of not a real action but a dream, the image of the action he imitates being even further from the truth, in consequence would be a still more imperfect poet. Following Plato one can come to no other conclusion however much Synesius may write that fables have their beginning in dreams, and that it is not unfitting that dreams should be their end as well.[3]

[1] *Discorsi del Poema Eroica*, in *Prose*, ed Francesco Flora, Milan, 1935, p. 325.

[2] *Ibid.*, pp. 324–25.

[3] *Ibid.*, pp. 323–24.

The ideas of Synesius are quite complex and systematically supported by a philosophy of the imagination. Tasso's reading of him is evidently just: "I even think that myths take their authority from dreams, as those in which peacock, fox, and sea hold converse. But these are small things compared with the independence of dreams. And although myths are a very small part of dreams, nevertheless they were approved by the sophists as a preparation for the work

But when it came to justifying his claim that epic poetry dealt with wonder even more than tragedy, his reasons were, on the one hand, that marvels were more "proper" to narrative, and on the other, that a reader can accept many things a spectator cannot consent to. His illustrations indicated that he is referring chiefly to the appearances of the gods in the ancient poets, and of angels in the moderns, as in Ariosto and Trissino.[1]

The rejection of Synesius, then, reduces to this, that the marvels peculiar to dreams are not matters for faith, or wonder.

The unreal world of Spenser's, this Faerie Land, in its arbitrariness so unlike the common world, with so many of its qualities suggesting the world of dreams and visions, making but little distinction between natural and supernatural, must lack this kind of wonder. Yet faith for Spenser was an immediate concern, if not in the neo-Platonic interest in dreams for divination, as for Synesius, at least for the works of divinity so clearly indicated in the story; and perhaps also because the fantastic itself, divorced from the ordinary, was thought to be closer to divinity, as the scene itself was more like Paradise, and the age more like the age of gold than ours.

So much one is immediately disposed to by the beauty of the scene and story and by the first thing we come to know about the first person in the poem, that he bears a cross and is moved by the love of Christ:

> A Gentle Knight was pricking on the plaine,
> Y cladd in mightie armes and siluer shielde,
> Wherein old dints of deepe wounds did remaine,
> The cruell markes of many' a bloudy fielde;

of eloquence. And for these men to whom the myth is the beginning of their art, the dream ought to be its appropriate end. And there is this in addition, that one has not worked the tongue in vain, as in the case of myths, but that he has become wiser in judgement." ("Concerning Dreams," in *The Essays and Hymns of Synesius*, tr. Augustine Fitzgerald, Vol. II, Oxford, 1930, p. 357.)

[1] *The Essays and Hymns of Synesius*, tr. Augustine Fitzgerald, Vol. II, Oxford, 1930, p. 334. See the note on page 199 below for further references in this matter.

Yet armes till that time did he neuer wield:
His angry steede did chide his foming bitt,
As much disdayning to the curbe to yield:
Full iolly knight he seemd, and faire did sitt,
As one for knightly giusts and fierce encounters fitt.

But on his brest a bloudie Crosse he bore,
The deare remembrance of his dying Lord,
For whose sweete sake that glorious badge he wore,
And dead as liuing euer him ador'd:
Vpon his shield the like was also scor'd,
For soueraine hope, which in his helpe he had:
Right faithfull true he was in deede and word,
But of his cheere did seeme too solemne sad;
Yet nothing did he dread, but euer was ydrad.

His religious desire and the desire of glory go together:

Vpon a great aduenture he was bond,
That greatest *Gloriana* to him gaue,
That greatest Glorious Queene of *Faerie* lond,
To winne him worship, and her grace to haue,
Which of all earthly things he most did craue;
And euer as he rode, his hart did earne
To proue his puissance in battell braue
Vpon his foe, and his new force to learne;
Vpon his foe, a Dragon horrible and stearne.

If religiousness gives the story its most intimate verisimilitude, the emphasis that belongs to the scene as a dream and as a song about a dream is developed as the circumstances that limit the adventures become clear.

After this introduction of the Knight we are told something about the Lady. She is sad, driven from her home as she is, and the Knight has come with her to revenge her. They are riding along, almost all their journey before them, there is nothing in sight that they note, and then a storm comes up and drives them to a shelter, a hideous storm over all the countryside:

> The day with cloudes was suddeine ouercast,
> And angry *Ioue* an hideous storme of raine
> Did poure into his Lemans lap so fast,
> That euery wight to shrowd it did constrain,
> And this faire couple eke to shroud themselues were fain.
>
> (I. i. 6)

That touch, the beating of the rain and the search for shelter, introduces the necessary idea, the idea at the origin of the suspense of the romance, the idea of isolation.

They find a wood, a wonderful place, protecting them from the rain. There is no light from the sky to reach them, and yet it is light enough to see by and the wood is full of the music of birds:

> Whose loftie trees yclad with sommers pride,
> Did spred so broad, that heauens light did hide,
> Not perceable with power of any starre:
> And all within were pathes and alleies wide,
> With footing worne, and leading inward farre:
> Faire harbour that them seemes: so in they entred arre.
>
> (I. i. 7)

The comfort of the idea of shelter, and the comfort, too, of the idea of isolation:

> And foorth they passe, with pleasure forward led,
> Ioying to heare the birdes sweete harmony,
> Which therein shrouded from the tempest dred,
> Seemd in their song to scorne the cruell sky.
>
> (I. i. 8)

> Led with delight, they thus beguile the way,
> Vntill the blustring storme is ouerblowne.
>
> (I. i. 10)

The next touch—they are lost:

> When weening to returne, whence they did stray,
> They cannot finde that path, which first was showne,
> But wander too and fro in wayes vnknowne,
> Furthest from end then, when they neerest weene,
> That makes them doubt, their wits be not their owne:
> So many pathes, so many turnings seene,
> That which of them to take, in diuerse doubt they been.
>
> At last resoluing forward still to fare,
> Till that some end they finde or in or out,
> That path they take, that beaten seemd most bare,
> And like to lead the labyrinth about;
> Which when by tract they hunted had throughout,
> At length it brought them to a hollow caue,
> Amid the thickest woods.
>
> (I. i. 10–11)

Whatever happens now, however they find a way out, in the rest of the story we know that the scene will always be as this, "the wandring wood, this *Errours den*" (I. i. 13), and they themselves always lone pilgrims, at the mercy of whatever terror and danger chance contrives for them—"the wandring wood."

As if the forest were not obstacle enough the Knight in his brashness must seek out danger. He notices a dark cave, and although Una pleads with him he will not let well enough alone and he pokes the hole until it brings out some monster:

> his glistring armor made
> A litle glooming light,

(the exaggeration even of horror)

> much like a shade,
> By which he saw the vgly monster plaine,
> Halfe like a serpent horribly displaide,
> But th'other halfe did womans shape retaine,
> Most lothsom, filthie, foule, and full of vile disdaine.
>
> (I. i. 14)

What happens now is the simple fascination of a strange event and a strange story, the small monsters flee from the unusual light, the Knight kills their mother, and then the infants suck up her blood until they burst from it.

The Knight, joined by the Lady, continues on again, still lost. The path they follow leads them out of the wood, but the old man they soon meet leads them to another:

> A little lowly Hermitage it was,
> Downe in a dale, hard by a forests side,
> Far from resort of people, that did pas
> In trauell to and froe.
>
> (I. i. 34)

And now the story takes us into Hellish adventures and increasing suspense. The Knight and Lady take refuge in this friendly hermit's cottage, and while they are innocently asleep, the hermit is revealed to us as a wicked magician. He goes to his books and charms, he summons a spirit and sends it beneath the earth to Morpheus to get from him a dream he will be able to make serve his purposes. So first he sends the dream to the Red Crosse Knight to trouble his sleep with lust, and then, having manipulated another spirit into the likeness of Una, he causes it to lie down wantonly beside the Knight to greet him as he wakes. And when the Knight discovers her boldness, he turns away in anger and sadness. And the magician tries again to separate the Knight from the Lady, and even to make him kill her. He turns his messenger-spirit into the likeness of a squire and puts him and the spirit resembling Una into a secret bed that he discovers to the Knight:

> Which when he saw, he burnt with gealous fire,
> The eye of reason was with rage yblent,
> And would haue slain them in his furious ire,
> But hardly was restreined of that aged sire.

Returning to his bed in torment great,
And bitter anguish of his guiltie sight,
He could not rest, but did his stout heart eat,
And wast his inward gall with deepe despight.
(I. ii. 5–6)

With the morning he rode away alone—

Will was his guide, and griefe led him astray.
(I. ii. 12)

The two are parted now, and fantastic adventures come to each, one after another. The Knight meets a stranger knight, fights with him and defeats him, and takes the defeated knight's lady along for dalliance. At a certain point he goes to make a garland for her of leaves from a tree, but plucking these blood falls from the torn branches and he hears a piteous crying, and then from the tree he hears the story of a knight and his lady turned into trees by a witch. The story fills the Knight with horror. And still others follow, and all come strangely unforeseen, without relief, almost as if there were some bad fate following him.

And worse happens. After a while he comes to a palace, and this is a magnificent place, and fearful, too, for there he sees a pageant of all the sins. He is challenged by an evil knight he is able to defeat, but he must still flee lest by other means he be thrown into a dungeon there where thousands had already perished.

Having escaped this he meets up with the false lady he had earlier taken from the first knight he defeated. He is again infatuated with her and through her duplicity he is made the prisoner of a Giant.

There is something almost hopeless in the succession of evils, hardly anything intelligible in their order, for even though we have the most perfect confidence in the ultimate safety of the Knight there is so little of the evil in this world he finds himself in that can be foreseen, still less forestalled, and so little indication of any way of rooting it out, of insuring that once one villain is destroyed there will not be any more to take his place. But all is not quite hopeless, however unreasoning the hope. The variety of the adventures, is, as it happens, pleasurable to contemplate, and for some reason we refuse to believe in disaster.

Una, too, as she sets out to find the Knight who has abandoned her meets strangeness after strangeness, and again the variety of things is delightful, although here hope of the happy event is stronger. Her wanderings at first are painful although she is without fear, and although she must soon escape from the magician who deceives her by taking the likeness of the Red Crosse Knight. Then, quite alone, falling asleep in the woods, a lion comes upon her all alone,

> Forsaken, wofull, solitarie mayd
> Farrē from all peoples prease, as in exile,
> In wildernesse and wastfull deserts strayd.
> (I. iii. 3)

The lion who came to devour remained to serve and protect her until an enemy knight killed him; and then, made captive, and all but in despair, she is rescued by a savage nation who worship her as a goddess.

All these adventures in their succession and their parallels somehow increase our interest, and the suspense in a quiet way is continually refreshed, not that each adventure is more extraordinary than the last but each is different, and there is too, the fear that with each adventure disaster for the Knight and the Lady is getting closer and closer. There is no let-down, and the reader sees no surcease, this fantastic world is so inhabited with enemies and the power of the enemies is so surely devilish, so far beyond the strength and wit of mortals to master once and for all.

There is one growing recognition, however, that makes the wanderings and adventures seem more than the mere senselessness of chance disaster. From the beginning there has been some fault on the knight's part, he has mistaken the object of his love. We did not know, nor is it certain that he did, that Una was his lady, his mistress, until he is revolted at what he thinks her licentiousness, and then he becomes jealous. And we did not know how much her love meant until he took up with Fidessa. As the story goes, he could not have known that this was a false appearance of Una, and he could not have known what magicians were working against him. But if the fault to begin with was not his, the mistake was and the suffering and the unfaithfulness. The result is—and this we know as we follow Una in her searching after him—that this becomes the story of parted lovers. Each new adventure separates them more and each danger Una faces increases the danger of both, the danger that they will never come together again. The threat of the loss of love and the desire that it be not lost join with the religious desires in convincing us of the reality of the wanderings of all such as are lost in the marvellous forest with its unending evil.

The Questing

I

The adventures of *The Faerie Queene* are fantastic by the nature of the conventions and circumstances developed in the history of romances. These set the tone for all that Spenser is to treat, and although the stories, the setting, and still other elements take their initial character from romantic traditions, there is yet by the nature of romances the opportunity for the expression of Spenser's particular religiousness, for the expression of the beliefs and aims of an Elizabethan Protestant. The history of romances shows their congeniality to stories of religion as well as of love, and in *The Faerie Queene* stories characteristic of romances and the conventional conception of the scene harmonize with the religious and amorous interests of the poet himself.

That the wood should be a wandering one, that there should be a world under the earth, that in the forest there should be no landmarks, no towns, no commerce, and that paths and roads should have no clear destination, all this signifies the existence of the scene according to other necessities than those of the ordinary world, and more according to the ways of the mind and desire. To be lost in Faerie Land does not mean to be lost from the highway to London or even to Tintagel, and the mission of this or that knight is against no such substantial a figure as epic or folktale figures, and the Lady is not even such a person as the Lady of Shalott, capable of dying. The forest of the poem is the image of the poet's own uncertainties. Spenser, introducing himself at the beginning—"I the man"—and keeping himself ever before us, in the image of the forest as in those of the questing knights, is part of the subject of the work. The imaginings he contrives are to help him lead his own thought and hope to certainty and satisfaction. W. P. Ker made the essential point, I think, about this kind of writing:

> The difference between the greater and lesser kinds of narrative literature is vital and essential, whatever names may be assigned to them. In the one kind, of which Aristotle knew no other examples than the *Iliad* and the *Odyssey*, the personages are made individual through their dramatic conduct and their speeches in varying circumstances; in the other kind, in place of the moods and sentiments of a multitude of different people entering into the story and working it out, there is the sentiment of the author in his own person; there is one voice, the voice of the story-teller, and his theory of the characters is made to do duty for the characters themselves. There may be every poetic grace, except that of dramatic variety; and wherever, in narrative, the independence of the characters is merged in the sequence of adventures, or in the beauty of the landscape, or in the effusion of poetic sentiment, the narrative falls below the highest order, though the art be the art of Ovid or of Spenser.[1]

A romance, told by someone who from the beginning has called himself to our attention as a reflective person apart from the story he is telling, cannot tolerate the simplicity that governs the stories of folklore, or such a story as that of Saint Brandan's marvellous journey to Paradise. As it is in *The Faerie Queene* there must be some sophisticated questioning or interpretation to accompany the incidents. The poet is always aware that there are two worlds throughout his poem, in every word, the world of what is said and the world of the mind that is telling us the story.

In drama and epic, I think Ker's studies show, the poet and the reader alike are drawn into the immediate scene, but in romances our very sympathy depends on the consciousness of our separation from what we are being told of. The poet, too, is outside, and the romance is told by someone about life within a place he himself has not yet entered. The circumstances of dream and vision literature seem to be the controlling facts, and the words of the *Romance of the Rose* offer a typical illustration of the self-consciousness of the narrator of romances:

[1] *Epic and Romance*, London, 1926, p. 33.

And whan I had a while goon,
I saugh a gardyn right anoon,
Ful long and brood, and euerydell
Enclosed was, and walled well
With highe walles embatailled,
Portraied without and wel entailled
With many riche portraitures.
And bothe the ymages and peyntures
Gan I biholde bysyly;
And I wole telle you redyly
Of thilk ymages the semblaunce,
As fer as I have remembraunce.

(135–46)

But way I couthe fynde noon
Into that gardyne for to goon.
Ne nought wist I if that ther were
Eyther hole or place where,
By which I myght have entre.
Ne ther was noon to teche me,
For I was al aloone i-wys,
For-wo and angwishis of this.
Till atte last bithought I me,
That by no weye ne myght it be
That ther nas laddre, or way to passe,
Or hole, into so faire a place.
Tho gan I go a full grete pas,
Envyronying evenè in compas
The closing of the square wall,
Tyl that I fonde a wiket small,
So shett that I ne myght in gon,
And other entre was ther noon.[1]

(513–30)

In the *Romance of the Rose* the dreamer's reflections and all the part he plays in the poem depend on his preserving the consciousness that he is in a certain sense outside the scene of the dream, and

[1] In Chaucer's translation.

through this, even when he apparently crosses the barrier, he is able to exploit all the parallels of waking and dreaming, of natural and supernatural, and of reality and symbol. The sense of this division is always kept before us, and as the romance is conducted towards the completion of the narrative, its unity is seen to depend on the success with which the two worlds are shown to be one—which is to say, in some way of interpretation.

Our interest in *The Faerie Queene* is founded on the same convention as it is also in the *Divine Comedy* and in *Pilgrim's Progress*. It is the account of the marvellous that stirs us in all these but we go beyond such interest only when we see how the strange and wonderful relate to truth, and when we see how the self-consciousness of the poet relates the marvellous to his own situation in reality. When Tasso concluded that the aim of romance and epic alike is wonder,[1] he meant, I think, wonder inspired with wisdom.

Tasso allows for no essential difference between romance and epic, but the different kinds of wonder he acknowledges are partly determined by the differences in the relation of the story-teller to his story. The *Iliad*, for example, told as something sung by the Muse, might correspond to the poem of revelation, just as Lovelich said the story of the Grail was written by God.[2] Dante's story

[1] See above page 55.

[2] but what Clerk is there So hardye,
that dar seyn, Other proven Openlye,
That God, Sethen his vp-Rysinge,
In Ony plase Made Ony wrytynge
Sauf Only this blessid Storye
Of Seint Graal ful Sekerlye.

(Henry Lovelich, *The Legend of the Holy Grail*, Part V [Early English Text Society, Extra Series, No. XCV (1905)], Bk. XXVII, ll. 346–51.)

The invocation of Pulci's *Morgante* is as instructive in this matter as Lovelich's remark:

In principio era il Verbo appresso a Dio,
ed era Iddio il Verbo e 'l Verbo lui;
questo era nel principio, al parer mio,
e nulla si può far sanza costui;

is told as a dream and a vision, and in this respect it is like the *Romance of the Rose.* Chrétien begins *Erec and Énide* by naming himself as the one who is to relate the story of the Round Table, and *Cligès* he begins by telling that this is a story he found in an old book. Ariosto's and Spenser's poems begin not too differently from these, and all from the nature of their beginnings must be

> però, giusto Signor, benigno e pio,
> mandami solo un degli angeli tui,
> che m'accompagni e rechimi a memoria
> una famosa, antica e degna istoria.
>
> E tu, Vergine, figlia e madre e sposa
> di quel Signor che ti dette la chiave
> del cielo e dell'abisso e d'ogni cosa,
> quel dí che Gabriel tuo ti disse *Ave*;
> perché tu se' de' tuoi servi pietosa,
> con dolce rime e stil grato e soave
> aiuta i versi miei benignamente
> e 'nsino al fine illumina la mente.

(*Il Morgante*, ed. George B. Weston, Bari, 1930):

> In the Beginning the Word was with God and God was the Word and the Word was God; thus it was in the beginning it seems to me and nothing could be done without Him. Therefore, Just Lord, kind and merciful as Thou art, send to me one of Thy Angels to be beside me, and to call back to my memory a famous, ancient, worthy story.
>
> And Thou, Virgin, daughter and mother and wife of that Lord that gave Thee the keys of Heaven and of the Abyss and of everything on that day that Gabriel said Hail! to Thee, because Thou art pitiful for Thy servants, gently help me in my verses with sweet rhyme and a pleasing and smooth style and light my mind to the very end.

For all Pulci's wit and scepticism the domination of the lyrical motive in the conduct of his poem is remarkable, especially considering that Ariosto also giving wit its range was able to achieve a style of detachment. The remarks of Illidio Bussani on Pulci's method help explain that poet's use of a romantic structure: "Il 'Morgante,' per poter essere compreso, deve essere studiato per

moving towards a different stirring and wonder, a different closeness to marvels.

If terms such as these indicate various ways of approaching wonder, in these methods and their various combinations one notices a constant reference to the writer or singer, or to inspiration. This is necessary because the structure and sense of the poem must be coherent, the marvels must be told in some way not to offend sense, and this means finally that the coherence must be tested not by some world of Platonic or Aristotelian ideals, or in the mind of God, but according to the coherence of all the teller's thoughts and interests. In the *Gerusalemme Liberata* Tasso's view of Armida and his view of Godfrey must betray no conflicts in his values. In *The Faerie Queene* Gloriana and Pastorella must embody qualities that will exist happily together in the poet's reasoning about the good of life. Because the writer remains part of the subject of the poem as the mind of a man bringing two worlds together, his own integrity must everywhere be manifest, because of the subject, and his solution of the religious problem made evident.

This means of course that in certain ambitious romances the teller must provide a means of clear interpretation, something to account for the significance or perhaps appeal of his fantastic matter. A poem told as a vision may require little comment, and depend chiefly on symbolic power, the symbols their own explanations or as near as explanations will get; or the vision may be turned into allegory and a commentary complexly interwoven.

quello che è: un'affermazione individuale. Se si consideri questo, se si consideri cioè che le vicende narrate dal poeta trovano la loro giustificazione a specchio non di una logica oggetiva, ma puramente soggetiva e che vivono non per sè, ma per il poeta, nel quale ritrovano l'unità ideale, tutte le inconseguenze, le dissonanze, le asperità del 'Morgante' si spiegano perfettamente e svaniscono; ed insieme con esse si dileguano, come nebbia mattutina, tutte quelle questioni che, basate sul pregiudizio e su falsi preconcetti, hanno per lungo tempo soffocato la voce di questa poesia schietta e vivace." "La povertà dei caratteri nel 'Morgante' è determinata dal fatto che tutti i personaggi del poema risentono del loro autore: chi più, chi meno, somigliano tutti al Pulci; essi si differenziano solo per dei caratteri esteriori, quali il loro fisico (uomini, donne, giganti) o il loro morale (Margutte, Gano), ma il fondo del loro carattere ci riporta sempre al carattere del Pulci." *Il Romanzo Cavalleresco in Luigi Pulci*, Turin, 1933, pp. 90, 85.

And these different ways may be mixed. As with Spenser all may be told as by an imaginary person, depending on inspiration, and all made true to his supposed character. Only rarely will it be as with Ariosto that the teller of the romance is a man in the daytime world.

> Ippolito, aggradir questo che vuole
> e darvi sol può l'umil servo vostro.
> Quel ch'io vi debbo, posso di parole
> pagare in parte e d'opera d'inchiostro;
> né che poco io vi dia da imputar sono,
> che quanto io posso dar, tutto vi dono.[1]
>
> (I. iii)

> Vouchsafe (O *Prince*) of most renowmed [*sic*] race,
> The ornament and hope of this our time,
> T'accept this gift presented to your grace,
> By me your servant rudely here in rime.
> And though I paper pay and inke, in place
> Of deeper debt, yet take it for no crime:
> It may suffice a poore and humble debter,
> To say, and if he could it shoulde be better.[2]

The coherence of such poems is as evident in their power to quicken feeling as in the communication of the thoughts of the writer, since his desire to unite divided worlds is itself part of the poem's subject and strength. It is here, I think, that we may recall those many writers who speak in the medieval phrase of "the love of the far-away." A work of the imagination, as the imagination itself, is by nature incapable of the perfect religious accomplishment, the certification of faith in the world of marvel and miracle. But there is always in the imagination the bitter passion, "l'amour de loin," the love of the difficult to attain, of the Earthly Paradise, of the perfection of the self—all that which creates the special romantic music, the note of yearning, "that haunting elegiac tone

[1] *Orlando Furioso*, ed. Santorre Debenedetti, Bari, 1928.

[2] *Orlando Furioso In English Heroical Verse*, by Sir John Harington [3rd edition, London], 1634.

or undertone which never fails in romance or homily to bring its sad suggestions of the vanity and transience of all things, of the passing away of pomp and splendour, of the falls of princes."[1] When this most lacks, the romance paradoxically becomes greatest. Then there ceases to be a poet or a dreamer to limit the truth of what is said, and the Muse or the Voice of God takes over and as it were the condition of grace, so long aspired to, allows the complete statement. A miracle may then be related as a fact and the story told by someone whose mind is not divided. The legend of Saint Brandan was so told. Somehow the ship had carried him and his friends, after many adventures, close to Paradise. ". . . they toke theyr shyppe and sayled eest xl. dayes, and at the xl. dayes ende it began to hayle ryght fast, and therwith came a derke myst, whiche lasted longe after, whiche fered Saynt Brandon and his monkes, and prayed to our Lord to kepe and helpe them. And than anone came theyr procuratour, and badde them to be of good chere, for they were come into the Londe of Byheest. And soon after that myst passed awaye, and anone they sawe the fayrest countree eestwarde that ony man myght se, and was so clere and bryght that it was an hevenly syght to beholde; and all the trees were charged with rype fruyte and herbes full of floures; in whiche londe they walked xl. dayes, but they coude se none ende of that londe; and there was alwaye daye and never nyght, and the londe attemperate ne to hote ne to colde. And at the last they came to a ryver, but they durst not go over. And there came to them a fayre yonge man, and welcomed them curtoysly, and called each of them by his name, and dyd grete reverence to Saynt Brandon, and sayd to them, 'Be ye now joyfull, for this is the londe that ye have sought.' "[2]

[1] W. P. Ker, *Essays on Medieval Literature*, London, 1905, p. 24.

[2] From the version of Saint Brandan's life printed in Wynkyn de Worde's edition of the *Golden Legend*, and reprinted from Thomas Wright's edition in *St. Brendan the Voyager, In Story and Legend*, Denis Donoghue, 2nd edition, Dublin, 1895, pp. 392–93.

The question of the development of romances from the accounts of the lives of the saints has not, I think, been studied sufficiently from the point of view of style and form. Many rich suggestions, however, have been made by Rosa Söder, *Die apokryphen Apostelgeschichten und die romanhafte Literatur der*

Such is the manner of narration and the note so different from the "haunting, elegiac tone" of Spenser and the aspiration of the words that end his poem—

Graunt me that Sabaoths sight.

II

The scene does not dominate romances to the degree that it singly determines the action or the characters. All the elements are important to each other according to the necessities of the original conception, yet we know that the scene has an importance of its own, and very often for the sense of foreboding and darkness. Whether the romance writer depends on symbol or allegory, or depends for power on the mere naming, the scene will always express more than the mention of facts might be expected to. This is part of what Stevenson meant when he referred to the suspense immediately created when a story begins on "the Malabar coast in a storm, with a ship beating to windward, and a scowling fellow of Herculean proportions striding along the beach."[1]

The scene of the forest had come to be the most memorable of all the romantic settings. Wyatt's phrase, "the hertes forrest,"[2] is a kind of epigram for it, and whether the hart be the lover, as in Wyatt and Spenser, or the great emperor Caesar as in Shakespeare,[3] or as in Malory, Christ,[4] the forest is the frame *par excellence* of the action, and the tremendous simplicity of Malory's words on

Antike, Stuttgart, 1932 (Würzburger Studien zur Altertumswissenschaft, Drittes Heft). Some suggestive points are also to be found in two other works: Hippolyte Delehaye, *Les Légendes Hagiographiques*, Brussels, 1927, and G. H. Gerould, *Saints' Legends*, Boston, 1916.

Miss Lois Whitney has studied the question of Spenser's knowledge of legends like those of the life of Saint Brandan in "Spenser's Use of the Literature of Travel in *The Faerie Queene*," *Modern Philology*, XIX (1921), 149–62.

1 R. L. Stevenson, "A Gossip on Romance," in *The Travels and Essays of Robert Louis Stevenson: Memories and Portraits*, New York, 1895, p. 327.

2 In the sonnet beginning, "The longe love, that in my thought doeth harbar"—*Collected Poems of Sir Thomas Wyatt*, ed. Kenneth Muir, London, 1949, p. 5.

3 *Julius Caesar*, III. i. 207.

4 *The Works of Sir Thomas Malory*, ed. Eugene Vinaver, Oxford, 1947, p. 999 (*Sir Galahad*).

Tristan, "whan he was madde in the foreyste,"[1] reach the centre of desolation. With whatever emphasis various stories give the dark woods its manifest symbolism in *La Queste del Saint Graal*, the simple, physical mystery in *Huon of Bordeaux*, the various kinds of allegory in Ariosto and Tasso and Spenser—there is a special perfectness in the choice of the image, and it may be in part that its force depends on the reminder of the forest of such as Blue Beard and the Sleeping Beauty, and the rest.

As so many before him, Spenser, too, required that the forest remain fantastic, the rivers unknown, the roads unmarked. For him it was to be neither the world of ideas and allegory nor the world of common sense, but the nameless world of the imagination itself. He had turned to this and away from the pastoral scene and the pastoral innocence towards a form and towards conventions where all the issues of life can be presented for solutions that may be seen to apply to Life itself and for instruction in the ways of greatness and religion. In the limitlessness of such a setting his knights and their wanderings would be towards their perfection. In Malory and Ariosto the questing may be ended in the discovery of the self,[2] but there, too, the forest is the necessary frame.

[1] *The Works of Sir Thomas Malory*, ed. Eugene Vinaver, Oxford, 1947, p. 513 (*Sir Tristram De Lyones*).

[2] M. Reto Bezzola has extended a generalization of this kind based on an analysis of the structure of Chrétien's romances by M. W. Kellermann ("Aufbaustil und Weltbild Chrestiens von Troys im Percevalroman," Halle: Niemeyer, 1936, in *Beihefte zur Zeitschrift für romanische Philologie*, Vol. LXXXVIII): "La conquête du monde, de la réalité par un héros, la réalisation de sa propre personnalité, s'accomplit normalement en deux phases: conquête facile d'abord, puisqu'elle n'est que celle d'un bonheur purement individuel (l'amour de Didon), conquête bien plus délicate et pénible ensuite qui dépasse l'individu et fait de lui une vraie personnalité, dans laquelle l'individu se double d'un membre et instrument de la société (conquête de l'Italie, de l'empire futur). L'Enée de Virgile est pleinement conscient de ces deux étapes. . . . Avec le Roman d'Eneas du XIIe siècle, malgré l'analogie de structure, nous sommes transportés dans un autre monde. L'esprit de l'Enée virgilien, dévoué complètement à la cause commune, à la gloire de la race future, n'est pas celui de la société courtoise, où le héros vise à la formation de sa propre personnalité, de son idéal de chevalier parfait. Déjà dans le Roman d'Eneas, cette formation s'accomplit à travers *l'amour*, Didon et Lavinie en représentant les deux phases. A Didon, dont la conquête

As the scene of the quest is the world the poet has imagined with the greatest liberty, his heroes are the person the poet is not and yet wishes to be. The questing figure, then, in the ancient phrase, partakes of God, and the adventures he meets in his quest are the means of trial and improvement. It will not always be as sometimes in *The Faerie Queene* that we shall be told in philosophic language of the degrees and stages of the knight's purification, or that we shall be able to estimate the progressive dangers of the evils he encounters. But as he overcomes one obstacle after another we always understand that he is thereby better able to meet the last.

The necessity of the scene, the forest, to such a person as a knight whose aim is in some part the perfection of himself, becomes clearer as we think of the nature of these individuals who are presented to us for our interest and sympathy and as we come to understand them as heroes of the poet's imagination, and limited by the terms of his desires. Tristan, Galahad, Launcelot, the Dreamer in the *Romance of the Rose*, the Red Crosse Knight are not to be understood or remembered by the name of an abstraction any more than the forest or the garden or the wandering wood. Nor are they, either, individuals of the kind most clearly realized in drama. Each is a person whose future is known to be another form of his present nature; there is that kind of simplification chiefly, and his purpose is quite consciously to realize his destiny. And this of course will be, if not felicity, that which is desired above everything else. However bitter life in the forest may be Tristan will accept it as the fulfilment of all his hopes—

Aspre vie meinent et dure;
Tant s'entraiment de bone amor
L'un por l'autre ne sent dolor.[1]

facile ne saurait retenir le héros, se substitue la dame lointaine— *l'amor de terra de lonh* de Geoffroi Rudel—Lavinie, la fiancée de l'adversaire, qui restera longtemps inaccessible, afin que l'amant ne triomphe qu'à travers les obstacles et les souffrances."—*Le sens de l'Aventure et de l'Amour* (*Chrétien de Troyes*), Paris: La Jeune Parque, 1947, pp. 84–5.

[1] Béroul, *Le Roman de Tristan*, ed. Ernest Muret, 4th edition revised by L. M. Defourques (Les Classiques Français du Moyen Age), Paris: Champion, 1947, ll. 1364–66.

For Galahad the heavenly transformation of his present joy will be a change without surprise: "And since it is so, fair gentle Lord, that you have accomplished my desire and allowed me to see what I have always longed to see, now I pray you, just as I am and in this great bliss, to permit me to pass from this earthly life to that in heaven."[1]

Shakespeare's Troilus expresses the substance of the chivalric faith, and this corresponds in all its depth, I think, to the faith and conscience of Spenser's knights:

> I am as true as truth's simplicity,
> And simpler than the infancy of truth.
> (*Troilus and Cressida*, III. ii. 176–77)

It is the same faith Antony has violated, and the words might also be Launcelot's or the Red Crosse Knight's:

> I have not kept my square; but that to come
> Shall all be done by the rule.
> (*Antony and Cleopatra*, II. iii. 6–7)

And Spenser needs to say to each knight errant as Oberon speaks to Huon, "I loue thee well by cause of the trouthe that is in the."[2]

[1] *The Quest of the Holy Grail*, tr. W. W. Comfort, London, 1926, p. 224; *La Queste del Saint Graal*, ed. Albert Pauphilet, Paris, 1949, p. 278.

[2] *The Bok of Duke Huon of Burdeux done into English of Sir John Bourchier, Lorde Berners*, ed. S. L. Lee (Early English Text Society, Extra Series: XL), London, 1883–84, p. 72.

La Queste del Saint Graal has been clearly related to Cistercian mysticism, and by such references it is probably correct to say, as Gilson does, "La quête de Dieu, c'est l'amour de Dieu en nous; mais l'amour de Dieu en nous, c'est notre participation finie à l'amour infini par lequel Dieu s'aime lui-même" (*L'Esprit de la Philosophie Médiévale*, Paris: J. Vrin, 1932, II, 73). I do not think one can so fix the philosophic context of chivalric ideas of honour and of truth to oneself, and it is perhaps sufficient for most purposes merely to reaffirm, by calling attention to the idea of the self in this way, the relationship of chivalry and romances. A certain consideration of these matters may be seen in the author's "*Pericles, Prince of Tyre:* A Study in the Dramatic Use of Romantic Narrative," *Shakespeare Quarterly*, IV (1953), 259–61.

Because love is so much the subject of the romance and each knight through that escapes his isolation, keeping the square also means deserving the love and trust of others, of Una or Angelica or Guenevere or Armida, or of God. To fail them is to fail himself, as it is also if he fails to keep or even to attain their love. Such failures drive Tristan and Launcelot mad. And in that poem where there is least of this perhaps quasi-mysticism that the Arthurian stories so often depend on, the *Orlando Furioso*, the madness is final, the great knight is lost and abandoned, and even in his mind there is no longer a direction.

Orlando's failure is tragic, but ordinarily in romances the failures that come from defects in the knight himself may be set right. As in *The Faerie Queene* the knight will accept whatever adventure offers itself, and in the fulfilment of the quest that is required of him we understand that this has not been the opportunity of chance but of grace. The errors are paid for at the cost of long experience: as Huon pays for the breaking of his word and Kay for his arrogance, as Launcelot for the wrong in his love of Guenevere, so Red Crosse and Guyon and the others pay for their mistakes. It seems, too, that for them as for Galahad, whatever his initial excellence, their trials better fit them for their greatest needs. The defeats the world itself administers are something else.

In most romances the enemies the forest harbours do not correspond intelligibly to defects in the knights that pass through it. As in *The Faerie Queene* the wicked humans will be, if not always Saracens, generally in some important way infidels, monstrously wicked people who have so far forgotten humanity and divinity that they lock up wives in dungeons, make robes of beards, or collect skulls. If not from another world, like wizards and witches, or at least linked to the lower regions by spirits and magic, they are monstrously inhuman, like Mordred. Although the dangers such beings represent are close enough to real evil, in the romances they are merely the casual dangers of a forest whose existence itself may be evil, nature submitted to the control of magicians, who are the great enemies. It is these who, although they lack the permanence of the gods, are omnipresent, and who, although defeated, return again and again to plague the knights.

The enchanters act as adversaries, and in *The Faerie Queene* one discovers no more sufficient reason for their enmity except that, not acknowledging the perfect sovereignty of God, they take to themselves the hope of ruling. There is no explanation, and the variety, the activity of evil remains mysterious, as vaguely defined as the enchanted forest itself, arbitrarily invented, sombre, hostile, all but indestructible, and lovable. Why the forest should be a labyrinth, why there should be monsters in it, there is no one to say. What matters is that the knight is sure in his faith that he will overcome the dangers and fulfil his aims, and the obstacles are, in the end, as Huon might say, delectable. But why this should be so, why the journey should be so intricate, there is no one to say.

Nevertheless, there are relations sometimes to be discovered in romances between the forest and the defects in the knights and ladies. The life in the Garden of Acrasia represents a phase of nature that is also a phase of weakness in humanity. In the story of Tristan and Iseult there is that extraordinary incident after their deaths that symbolizes not only the faithfulness of the lovers but the nature of their bonds: "Puis, les deux amants furent mis au tombeau, et l'on raconte qu'Isolt, la femme de Tristan, fit enterrer Tristan et Isolt en deux tombes, des deux côtés de l'église, afin qe même après leur mort ils fussent séparés. Mais il arriva qu'un chêne ou telle autre espèce d'arbre germa de chaque côté du tombeau, et les deux arbres crûrent si haut qu'ils entrelacèrent leurs ramures au-dessus du toit: par là l'on peut voir quelle fut la grandeur de leur amour."[1] Here the heart and the forest are intermingled. But most fascinating of all is the enchanted forest of the *Gerusalemme Liberata*, where, as De Sanctis said, the forest is the poet himself. "His enchanted wood, like his enchanted garden and palace, is the work of an artist who poses it himself and for his own purposes. The conception of the enchanted wood is not new; it is the well-known wood of false appearances, the wood of error, of the passions. But the thing that is very original in Tasso

[1] Translated by Bédier from the Norse imitation of the romance of Thomas (*Le Roman de Tristan par Thomas*, Paris (Société des Anciens Textes Français), 1902, I, 416, note).

is his treatment of it. The wood is himself in miniature, the whole of his world of elegy and idyll, condensed and emphasized."[1]

For Spenser the greatest evils are of one's own creation, and most often the dangers of the forest are only likenesses to the darkness in the soul, at once hindering the aspirations of his heroes and providing the means by which they achieve their realization. The wandering wood is sometimes the wood of the passions, as is the Garden of Acrasia, but normally it has no other definition than in the vastness and variety of the imagination.

III

now I begin
To tread an endlesse trace, withouten guyde,
Or good direction, how to enter in,
Or how to issue forth in waies vntryde,
In perils strange, in labours long and wide,
In which although good Fortune me befall,
Yet shall it not by none be testifyde.
(VI. i. 6)

However beautiful the world Calidore will enter, the poet who tells his story is evidently terrorized not only by the thought of the failure of love but also by perfidy and injustice. Whatever the truth within himself, or whatever the love that moves him, Calidore and Guyon as much as Arthur or Arthegall are sooner or later meeting with the greater questions of society and in particular the question of justice. It is indeed to be expected that what begin as the simplest romantic stories will extend themselves into more complex patterns and will encompass in their matter the consideration of the knight as a member of society as well as in his character as a lover and a follower of Christ. In Spenser every effort is made to integrate all activity within the purity of the initial conception of the questing knight. The same need to

[1] Francesco De Sanctis, *History of Italian Literature*, tr. Joan Redfern, New York, 1931, p. 662.

extend the range of romantic action is ironically testified to in De Meung's continuation of the *Romance of the Rose*, where the satire rests not on the wrongness of the initial conception of the dream in its claim to bear an analogy to life but in its inadequacy.

In short, the story of a questing knight in a fantastic world becomes the story of many knights when the romantic and dream conventions are put to the service of the most aspiring writers. So it is that a story in Spenser beginning with a forlorn lady and a lamb and a dwarf coming into a king's hall develops into a series of stories about several knights, and in the end it will tell us something about all the different virtues required of men in our world. The necessity for such amplification of the narrative structure had long been recognized by the writers of romances, and in this as in so many other matters Spenser was agreeing with the wisdom of a tradition. The complexity was in his chief model, of course, Ariosto, but it was also in the *Queste del Saint Graal* and the *Morte D'Arthur*, and some analysis of the conduct of these two works helps illuminate, I think, Spenser's planning of his poem.

There is variety in the landscape of *La Queste del Saint Graal*, forests, meadows, waste land, rock cliffs. As the adventures of the knights are told to us the scenes change quickly, and generally there is little precise detail and but little description for the sake of vividness, except perhaps in the presentation of the *Terre Gaste* where the allegory is especially demanding. Most of the adventures take place in forests, different ones, vaguely apart, and hardly differing except in their extent. There is nowhere the sense of the confined, single scene of the *Romance of the Rose*. All this signifies, as Pauphilet observed, that "Le monde des idées est le seul qui existe vraiment et qui soit décrit dans la *Queste*."[1]

The secret is told us close to the beginning of the book: "This Quest is not a quest for earthly things, but is to be the search for the deep secrets and confidences of Our Lord and for the great mysteries which the High Master will show openly to that fortunate knight whom he has elected among all the other knights of earth to be his servant. To him he will reveal the great marvel

[1] Albert Pauphilet, "Études sur la Queste del Saint Graal attribuée à Gautier Map," Paris, 1921, p. 175.

of the Holy Grail and will show him what mortal heart could not conceive nor the tongue of earthly man utter."[1]

And yet the presence of such a world as we see and touch, and of the forest especially, perhaps as its symbol, is one of the impressive elements in the power of this romance. As if its constant presence, its pressingness, made no description necessary, and as if, somewhat as in fairy tales, one needs and is indeed compelled to mention it continually.

The story begins with the wonder that comes from an almost sacred formula: "On the eve of Pentecost, when the companions of the Round Table had come to Camelot and had heard mass, and when the tables were about to be set at the noon hour, there entered the hall a very fair damsel on horseback. It was evident that she had come in great haste, for her horse was still all in a sweat." She said nothing except to ask that Launcelot be pointed out to her, and then she requested his service. He blindly agreed to go with her: " 'And what is your need of me?' he inquired. 'That you shall soon see,' she replied. 'Then in God's name,' he said, 'I will gladly go.' "[2]

"And when they had gone forth from Camelot, they rode until they came into the forest."[3]

And so it is almost everywhere: "Meanwhile Launcelot rode in pursuit of the knight hither and thither through the forest, following no trail or pathway, but going at random where chance took him. His regret was that he could see neither in the distance nor near at hand any path to follow, for the night was very dark."[4] "So Perceval stayed with his aunt all that day. And on the morrow, as soon as he had heard mass and was armed, he went away and rode all day through the forest which was so vast that he met neither man nor woman."[5] " 'Launcelot, this forest is very wide and pathless; a knight may well travel for a day without finding house or habitation.' "[6]

Some details give for a moment a sense of particular reality—

[1] *The Quest of the Holy Grail*, tr. Comfort, p. 15; *La Queste*, ed Pauphilet, p. 19.
[2] *Ibid.*, p. 1; *Ibid.*, p. 1.
[3] *Ibid.*, p. 1; *Ibid.*, p. 2.
[4] *Ibid.*, p. 46; *Ibid.*, p. 57.
[5] *Ibid.*, p. 65; *Ibid.*, p. 81.
[6] *Ibid.*, p. 116; *Ibid.*, p. 145.

a small meadow in the midst of the forest, a crossroad, a castle, a monastery, islands as it were in the woods something like the islands Saint Brandan came across in his pathless journey. Occasionally, as when we come to a hermitage, outside the forest in a valley, we are warmed with the thought of human company, and so reminded of the loneliness of the Quest.[1] And except for such occasional quickenings the forest is always about to become the great waste of the world, the Forest Gaste. "Comme le désert, la forêt est un lieu sans ressources, lieu d'erreurs, lieu de mort. Souvent même elle est appelée 'desvoiable,' sans chemin, tandis que Jésus dit: 'Je suis la Voie' ["Ego sum via, veritas et vita," parole citée d'ailleurs dans la *Queste*.] On voit de reste avec quelle facilité un esprit habitué aux transpositions mystiques pouvait tirer de là un beau symbole des erreurs du péché et de la perdition de l'âme. Aussi, pour montrer la différence entre une 'bonne âme' et un pécheur, la *Queste* nous montre-t-elle l'un regagnant la grand'route, tandis que l'autre reste errant dans la forêt."[2]

Brandan's journey was guided by a plainly declared faith; the dreamer in the *Romance of the Rose* faced a specific problem, how to get into the Garden. But in these forests and valleys, this image of the world, the cause and purpose of the adventures of the knights is not so plainly defined for the reader, although the Grail is known to be the object of the Quest.

If the knight's response is always as immediate as Launcelot's to the desolate maid, this readiness but intensifies the mysteriousness of a journey taken by no known paths, where chance seems always to be the guide: "Sallying forth from the castle they took leave of each other as had been agreed, and entered the forest at divers places where they saw it to be thickest and wherever

[1] "When he had left the scene of the conflict, the Good Knight rode aimlessly until he came at night within two leagues of Corbenyc. And it chanced that night overtook him when he was in front of a hermitage. When he noticed that night had fallen, he dismounted and knocked at the hermit's door until it was opened to him. When the hermit saw him to be a knight-errant, he welcomed him, stabling his horse, and helping him to lay aside his arms. After he was disarmed, he gave him to eat of such fare as God had provided."—*The Quest*, p. 161; *La Queste*, pp. 197–98.

[2] Pauphilet, *Études sur La Queste del Saint Graal*, p. 113.

they saw there was no road or path."[1] And again: "Meanwhile Launcelot rode in pursuit of the knight hither and thither through the forest, following no trail or pathway, but going at random where chance took him."[2]

Such blind wanderings would be of much less interest, however, did they not follow from some oath instead of being in the mere spoiling for adventure. The interest is increased by the sacredness of the oath. The search itself may be blind, the maiden's need unknown, and it is certain enough that the nature of the Grail is but partly understood. But the holiness of the search is sure, as sure as Launcelot in engaging himself unquestioningly in the maiden's errand, and as sure as Gawain, young and rash and swearing the oath that will be the end of the company of the Round Table: "Wherefore, for my part I make this vow, to enter tomorrow without delay upon the Quest and to prosecute it for a year and a day, and longer yet if need be; and I will not return to court for any reason whatsoever until I have seen it more clearly than it has been manifested to me here, if peradventure it be destined that I can behold it. And if it be destined otherwise, I will return."[3]

The holiness of the obligation must be matched by the purity of the knight, for the Grail is only to be seen by two who are virgin and one who is chaste. More comprehensively than *Comus* this romance expounds "the sage and serious doctrine of Virginity," "condition première de la sainteté, source de toutes les vertus. . . . la pureté absolue des âmes, dont la virginité corporelle n'est qu'une des conditions et comme le signe matériel."[4]

The doctrine is of course mystical. The desire of the knight, and of the story-teller, is a desire for heaven, in some absolute conception quite different from mere religiousness, although in the

1 *The Quest of the Holy Grail*, p. 20; *La Queste*, p. 26.

2 *Ibid.*, p. 46; *Ibid.*, p. 57. "Quand la légende du Graal eut pris essentiellement la forme d'une 'quête' générale, il devint plus évident que jamais que nul chemin connu ne devait conduire au Graal, et que seul le hasard, ou une volonté surnaturelle, y pouvait soudain amener le chevalier aventureux."—A. Pauphilet, "Au Sujet du Graal," *Romania*, LXVI (1940), 292.

3 *Ibid.*, p. 13; *Ibid.*, p. 16.

4 Pauphilet, *Études sur la Queste*, pp. 39–40.

end Galahad can find only the words of any Christian; "I pray you, just as I am and in this great bliss, to permit me to pass from this earthly life to that in heaven."[1]

The quality of the faith is of course the secret of the structure of the entire romance, of its setting, the forest that is more a presence than a range of trees; the ideas that are more real than a sword sheathed in a rock; the adventures that are more meaningful than declared allegories. This faith and its peculiarity are the inspiration of the romance, and what it is to prove. And the form the romance takes following necessities created by the conception itself has been so well described by the late Professor Pauphilet that I feel it is right to quote him at length, and especially because so many of the features of the structure of the romance as he describes them are also those of the *Orlando Furioso* and *The Faerie Queene:*

Comme notre romancier symbolisait par la "quête" du saint Graal la recherche de Dieu, c'est-à-dire la grande aventure collective de l'humanité, et comme il résumait en quelques personnages typiques la diversité qu'une telle aventure fait paraître entre les hommes, le plan qui s'imposait à lui était d'écrire une série de biographies parallèles. La vie morale, l'effort vers Dieu, est chose essentiellement personnelle, individuelle; puisque par hypothèse les héros de la *Queste* représentent les divers types de chrétiens, il fallait les décrire séparément et montrer chacun suivant sa propre voie, bonne ou mauvaise, dans la solitude de sa conscience. Aussi la *Queste* présente-t-elle le plus ordinairement un seul personnage à la fois. Mais pour que la comparaison des bons et des mauvais fût instructive, il fallait qu'elle fût en quelque sorte continuelle et que le lecteur ne perdît jamais personne de vue trop longtemps. De là la nécessité de passer fréquemment d'un héros à l'autre, de couper chacune des biographies en chapitres assez brefs. Enfin, quelle que soit l'infinie variété de la conduite humaine, elle aboutit à l'inévitable alternative du salut ou de la damnation; Dieu rassemble finalement ceux dont les mérites se ressemblent. Aussi les destinées des élus, séparées pendant le temps des épreuves, doivent-elles se rejoindre au moment des récompenses, qui est la fin naturelle du livre. Ainsi la trame narrative de ce roman est

[1] *The Quest*, p. 224; *La Queste*, p. 278.

faite de ces récits biographiques qui, pareils à des fils diversement colorés, forment tour à tour le dessin principal, puis se perdent, reparaissent, s'entrecroisent, et dont les plus brillants seuls se réunissent enfin pour former un dernier et magnifique motif. Ce mode de composition a été justement appelé le "principe de l'entrelacement." On le retrouve bien ailleurs que dans la *Queste*. Le *Lancelot* proprement dit le pratique, ainsi que l'a démontré M. F. Lot, avec une rare maîtrise; les récits interrompus un instant y sont toujours exactement repris, la concordance des temps entre les aventures y est observée et, malgré le désordre apparent du conte, ses retours en arrière, toute sa complexité touffue, si bien faite pour égarer lecteurs et auteur, la chronologie y est parfaitement nette et sûre.[1]

If Spenser's management of the adventures of several knights is nearly as systematic as this, Malory's compilation is in the nature of things a more casual variety of knights and adventures. Yet here, too, as it seems that Caxton saw, there was the stuff of unity. And there is in the *Morte D'Arthur* in the presentation of the scene still something else to help, by comparison, to bring into clearer view some of the methods of Spenser's presentation.

The Winchester manuscript of the *Morte D'Arthur* makes it easy to observe some of the differences of substance and treatment in the various stories Malory was translating and adapting. A contrast between his version of *La Queste del Saint Graal* and the received text, or his adaptation of the Tristan and Iseult story with some other accounts shows plainly what virtues he chose to emphasize, and how he preferred to regard the setting. And allowing for all the differences that by the nature of things come into a compilation, there is still in these many stories much of commonness, matter for unity, and something close to a consistency of view. The reader, of course, will often bring to so complex a work a disposition to believe that everything relates to everything else although a scrupulous examination might show many failures of this and that to join. But ordinarily the disposition to read the work as a whole, to consider it one, has been so strong that the

[1] *Études sur la Queste*, pp. 162–3. This use of the word "entrelacement" M. Pauphilet credits to Ferdinand Lot, *Étude sur le Lancelot en Prose*, Paris, 1918. The second chapter of M. Lot's book is devoted to this matter.

material and the persuasion of the style, if nothing else, have almost won the point. And even if, in the end, such a submission could not be proved to be the wisest approach to these writings, from other points of view there is much to learn in at least considering the collection as the work of a single writer.

Of all that Malory's writing tells about, its most constant subject is the unending performance of duty. Launcelot, Tristan, Galahad, all at any moment as for most of the moments of their lives are performing gallant deeds, for love, for God, for honour's sake. From time to time we learn that for these knights there is some surcease, with their mistresses or in feasting or in convalescence or even in prison. Sometimes there are long sea-journeys when little enough happens, although there is no journey on land that is not interrupted by numbers of incidental combats, all in following the code of honour.

In this life of missions that are accomplished only to be succeeded almost immediately by others, there is more than anything else an almost endless traversing of forests. In other romances the references seem less crowded. Here, although there are occasional highways, marshes, deserts, rivers, lakes and seas, all are hardly more than open places in one vast woods. "So at the laste they com into a grete foreste that was named the contrey and foreste of Arroy, and the contrey is of stronge adventures."[1] "And on the morne the damesell toke hir leve and thanked the knyght, and so departed and rode on hir way untyll they come to a grete foreste. And there was a grete ryver and but one passage, and there were redy two knyghtes on the farther syde to lette the passage."[2]

Encounters with friends or enemies seem at first accidental, and yet there is something in the atmosphere that suggests fate. Thanks to the prophecies of Merlin and others, the curious circumstances by which Arthur came to possess his kingdom, the career of Galahad from the beginning, and many other matters, we are conscious of mysterious, complicated plans in the scheme of things. It is, for example, no surprise to come upon a hermit who had been living in the forest for years, presumably out of touch

[1] *The Works of Sir Thomas Malory*, ed. Eugene Vinaver, Oxford, 1948, p. 162 (*Gawain, Ywain and Marhalt*). [2] *Ibid.*, p. 301 (*Sir Gareth of Orkeney*).

with the whole world, and yet immediately that Launcelot speaks to him he recognizes him, knows what has happened in his past life, and knows what is to come. Something in incidental matters, perhaps in the setting, also communicates the sense of fate. "And as sone as he was in the foreste, the kynge saw a grete harte before hym. 'Thys hart woll I chace' seyde kynge Arthure."[1]

A kind of vagueness is as noticeable as the suggestions of fatality, something partly fantastic, partly the merely unexplained, all perhaps adding up to the usual Celtic way of looking at the supernatural, telling a story about a sword in a rock in such a way that one hardly dare ask questions about it. There are other justifications, though, for the lack of clarity in these matters, as when King Pellynor said, "God may well fordo desteny"[2]—an idea few stories could make plain.

If such vagueness is partly an intellectual difficulty, partly a poetic device, there is a comparable and perhaps related vagueness in the communication of the states of character and the states of passion. Launcelot and Guenevere are profoundly faithful in their love and yet we are not led to any imaginative sharing of the depth of passion that must have been there. Yet we understand their faithfulness, and perhaps this is because instead of the psychologic method of many romances Malory here has something of the epic style, like Homer telling us about Penelope. But this cannot account for an absence of feeling in the words, in the figures of speech, remembering as it is so easy to do some such speech as that of William of Orange to his wife: "J'en fais le serment: jusqu'à mon retour je ne changerai ni de chemise, ni de braies, ni de chausses, et ne me laverai point la tête. Je ne mangerai ni chair, ni ragoût; je ne boirai ni vin ni breuvage épicé. L'eau seule apaisera ma soif, et je n'aurai d'autre nourriture que ce gros pain où l'on trouve la paille. Je ne coucherai point sur la plume et n'aurai pour abri ni draps ni courtines, rien que la couverture de ma selle et la robe que j'aurai emportée."[3]

[1] *The Works of Sir Thomas Malory*, ed. Eugene Vinaver, Oxford, 1948, p. 42 (*Merlin*). [2] *Ibid.*, p. 119 (*Torre and Pellynor*).

[3] The translation of F. Guessard and A. De Montaiglon in their edition of *Aliscans* (*Les Anciens Poëtes de la France*, Paris 1870, p. xxiii).

Nor are there words in Malory so simply strong as are said of Huon of Bordeaux—"for he hadde so great desire to se his wyf and his child that he put from hym all fere of dethe."[1] In the accounts of Launcelot's and Tristram's madnesses we see that they are distraught, and admiring them so much we have enough sympathy to imagine part of their distress, but we are not required, as in Bédier's version of the Tristan story, or as in Ariosto, to recall how deeply the madness is our own.

Where the vagueness is most interesting and perhaps most effective is in the relation of the story of the Holy Grail. For once there are many particulars, in the description of material, of strange lights, details about the food brought to men in a dungeon, and here the particular description emphasizes the mystery of the Grail itself, its invisibleness and all the strangeness about the search for it. Here, of course, the Christian mystery is the substance of the story and may well agree with whatever Malory's intuition of the unspeakable relations of God and destiny, and his ideas about fate and King Arthur's happening upon that place in the forest where the hart then was.

And if it is true that the setting, the omnipresent forest, is part of the fatefulness of the work, the quality of its mystery and hidden power emphasizes what appears to be the fundamental disposition of the knights of the story—"what aventure shalle falle to me, be it lyfe or dethe, I wille take the adventure that shalle come to me."[2] This is what the quest has become for Malory, not so much the seeking of adventure, for the assertion of courage or strength, or for the righting of wrongs, or for the salvation of souls—although all these motives are to be recognized in various actions—but the quest is for Malory above all else, more than a service voluntarily assumed for God, the way a knight fulfils the demands of destiny. From such an idea Spenser was to go on easily to declare the power of Providence, even in love:

[1] *The Bok of Duke Huon of Burdeux done into English of Sir John Bourchier, Lorde Berners*, ed. S. L. Lee (Early English Text Society, Extra Series: XL), London, 1882–4, p. 428.

[2] *The Works of Sir Thomas Malory*, p. 89 (*The Knight with the Two Swords*).

It was not, *Britomart*, thy wandring eye,
Glauncing vnwares in charmed looking glas,
But the streight course of heauenly destiny,
Led with eternall prouidence, that has
Guided thy glaunce, to bring his will to pas.
(III. iii. 24)

Launcelot seems a more important figure than Galahad or Tristan in the whole collection of stories. He is a grown man with none of the peculiar distinctions of the saintly and not, perhaps, cursed, as Tristan seems to be. Above all he is a man who who will always rely upon himself. And this, I suppose, is why all the others know they can depend upon him. There is something peculiarly touching about the chance encounter with a maiden just after he had waked from a sleep: "And so sir Launcelot departed, and by adventure he com into the same foreste there he was takynge his slepe before; and in the myddys of an hygheway he mette a damesel rydynge on a whyght palfrey, and there eythir salewed other."[1] As if in the whole world she had come upon the one person, alone as he is, to dare whatever her need requires.

The separate story of *Launcelot du Lake* accentuates the loneliness of the kind of man he is—mature, perfected, and with a kind of abnegation, a peculiar kind, as of that belonging to one whose fidelity to his mistress, placing him as it does in a world from which even his monarch is excluded, confines him in loyalty to a certain being, Guenevere, in a society apart.

His generosity seems to exist only in itself, with so little reference to any other trust than the trust in himself: a man with his capacities for fatherhood, knighthood, royalty, out of some fantastic kindness letting Sir Kay ride off in his, Launcelot's, armour, so that no enemy will dare attack him; his refusing love to so many beautiful women; the adventures he undertakes time after time when there is no one who could do him like service. This is an almost sacrificial life except that it is foolish to speak of generosity as sacrifice. "And so he rode into a grete foreste all

[1] *The Works of Sir Thomas Malory*, p. 264 (*Sir Launcelot du Lake*).

that day, and never coude fynde no hygheway."[1] "Than seyde sir Launcelot, 'I am in a queste that I muste do myselff alone.' "[2] Calidore once said the same thing:

> But I am bound by vow, which I profest
> To my dread Soueraine, when I it assayd,
> That in atchieuement of her high behest,
> I should no creature ioyne vnto mine ayde.
>
> (VI. ii. 37)

This is perhaps the centre of Malory's conception of the stories he tells about life, his conception of the knightly life. For there is an ever-present need in the world for such men as this, he seems to say, this monster-ridden world, with pathless forests, and where men from envy or madness or some injury to their pride cast others into prison to die, and where for all reasons many people of excellence are doomed to interminable despair. Launcelot as any other ignorant of his enemy and his enemy's crimes, more often than not, is sure of one thing, of himself and of the need to be true to himself. "Framed of the firm truth of valour," in being true to himself he is like an instrument of fate, although we can never be sure that he is that. The answer for Launcelot as for Huon of Bordeaux and for Spenser, is the same: " 'Sir,' he seyde, 'I have nothyng done but that me ought for to do.' "[3] " 'Madame,' seyde sir Launcelot, 'I shall take the adventure that God woll gyff me.' "[4] From this, too, Spenser goes to his own great doctrine:

> His be the praise, that this atchieu'ment wrought,
> Who made my hand the organ of his might;
> More then goodwill to me attribute nought:
> For all I did, I did but as I ought.
>
> (II. i. 33)

[1] *The Works of Sir Thomas Malory*, p. 259 (*Sir Launcelot du Lake*).
[2] *Ibid.*, p. 449 (*Lamerok de Galys*).
[3] *Ibid.*, p. 274 (*Sir Launcelot du Lake*).
[4] *Ibid.*, p. 1066 (*The Fair Maid of Astolat*).

These poems and stories may help us think of *The Faerie Queene* as a work, in which the poet regards himself as relating his own pilgrimage ("a wandering pilgrimage," it may be, as the *Daphnaida* calls it), or as some blind casting of himself upon the sea, as Tristan, for the wind and tides to take him where they will. And to the degree that there is in Spenser's poem and in these works what one may think of as essential matters in the romantic tradition, one might generalize, for the sake of reading Spenser, like this:

All is part of one conception, the isolation of humans moving forward in an unfamiliar world, but moving forward urged from within with the desire for glory and love. Those moving towards glory may know where they are going, although the roads they follow they come across by chance, and the journey is not measured by miles or days; those moving after love wander blindly but no less faithfully. And the single conception a poet such as Spenser holds to is the one in which the movement towards divinity and the wandering of the lover are seen to be part of the divinity of man, that very essence that God looks to to care for, which with grace He guides and preserves.

In the stories of *The Faerie Queene* (as in the *Mutabilitie* cantos) the scene, the universe, is not important except as something arbitrarily controlled to establish the relationships of men to each other and to God and to those they love. Glory is achieved not alone in the fulfilment of a man's own nature but also in helping to purify the relations between men in society (destroying injustice, calumny, deceit) for only in a just and perfect society do even love and marriage establish a permanent relationship (the Red Crosse Knight and many another must leave after his betrothal to take up other quests). Restlessness is everywhere.

The Italians

As we read *The Faerie Queene*, turning our thought back now and then to remember what has happened before, we see that what has carried our interest forward with the music has been something of the trials of holiness and temperance, certain beautiful scenes, suspense that is from time to time attendant on the hideousness of deceit and evil, here and there a detail from the innumerable combats, the charm of a garden, and figures of speech or lines that permanently hold the mind—

Yet will I not fro mine owne loue remoue.

(III. i. 28)

Loe this dead corpse, that lies here vnderneath,
The gentlest knight, that euer on greene gras
Gay steed with spurs did pricke, the good Sir *Mordant*
was.

(II. i. 49)

If we try to remember the narrative in its proper sequence and the phases of the allegory, we are lost unless we undertake a feat of memory. But if we let our minds play over the work, not to simplify but to order what we naturally retain, I think we are most likely to think first of a great forest full of light. In the wide spaces of this forest knights and squires are riding over turf, seeing each other from a long way off, coming together and clashing. At one place there will be a lady accompanied by a protector, at another we shall see one who is fleeing a pursuer, and at still another point one who is forlorn and lost. At great distances from each other there are castles rising within walls and now and then a cottage. There are not many wild creatures here, a single lion, a band of satyrs, and, of course, a dragon, nor are there many flowers and shrubs to be recalled except from the tapestries in one or another of the castles, and we are more likely to remember a tree carved in stone or metal to ornament a magic garden than particular ones in the forest. In remote islands or hidden flowery places we remember creatures who are like the goddesses of love and beauty, splendid and magnificent or simple and gentle. Sometimes there are dark places in the forest, when we are taken to visit the cave of a monster. And there are places also where some knight has lain down, consumed with care. Then, in a dream or through some other more mysterious circumstance, the darkness is lit up as if by magic.

Thinking back over all that we have read, it is not the narrative and not an articulated theme but the luxuriance of the life in the forest that comes back to us most forcefully, and a sense of the vitality of life in the forest and in men and women, the luxuriance of it and the variety. And seeing how much this impression dominates our memory of the poem, we are led by the fragment of the seventh book to understand even more surely how the idea of variety is itself much of the substance of the poem, not only in presenting a comprehensive scene but as the sign of the wealth and beauty and attraction of the world.

In the last cantos Jove at first wants to strike Mutabilitie down when she comes to his court to defy him, but when he sees her beauty he holds back:

he shooke
His Nectar-deawed locks, with which the skyes
And all the world beneath for terror quooke,
And eft his burning levin-brond in hand he tooke.

But, when he looked on her louely face,
In which, faire beames of beauty did appeare,
That could the greatest wrath soone turne to grace
(Such sway doth beauty euen in Heauen beare)
He staide his hand.

(VII. vi. 30–31)

Which is as much to say that the poet also has so felt the authority of change, that he recognizes the beauty of variety in all its tremendous power.

The solution that is finally presented in the *Mutabilitie* cantos to all the questions about change and eternity is plainly Christian, although such implications were not always necessary in what had gone before, in the praise of beauty and variety elsewhere in the progress of the poem. But it may be said that all the love of mortality expressed in the other books was of a nature to demand this and only this conclusion, or else to admit a contradiction in belief where there would have been no way to bind the ideas of the poem all together.

Mutabilitie insists upon a hearing, and the case is heard on a hill so beautiful the gods once chose it as a place for them to play on. Nature holds the court, a figure at once terrible, and we are led to suppose, awful with beauty.

> For, with a veile that wimpled euery where,
> Her head and face was hid, that mote to none appeare.
>
> That some doe say was so by skill deuized,
> To hide the terror of her vncouth hew,
> From mortall eyes that should be sore agrized;
> For that her face did like a Lion shew,
> That eye of wight could not indure to view:
> But others tell that it so beautious was,
> And round about such beames of splendor threw,
> That it the Sunne a thousand times did pass,
> Ne could be seene, but like an image in a glass.
>
> (VII. vii. 5–6)

After her came the procession of the seasons and then the months, Day and Night, Life and Death, and by this display Mutabilitie made the point that Nature is subjected to change, and Spenser himself has made the inevitable confession, that he loves all changing, mortal things too much, and they are betraying him:

> When I bethinke me on that speech whyleare,
> Of *Mutability*, and well it way:
> Me seemes, that though she all vnworthy were
> Of the Heav'ns Rule; yet very sooth to say,
> In all things else she beares the greatest sway.

Which makes me loath this state of life so tickle,
And loue of things so vaine to cast away;
Whose flowring pride, so fading and so fickle,
Short *Time* shall soon cut down with his consuming sickle.
(VII. viii. 1)

The great renunciation that follows is only partly the renunciation of earthly love, for the commitments to mortality have gone too deep to allow that now. It is a prayer for transmutation and redirection. Change, Nature argued, was not a movement towards decay but was the method of perfection. But man, whose time is limited, cannot take the comfort he requires from such a paradox, for the fulfilment is beyond the reach of a lifetime. Since he requires, he thinks, the fulfilment his desires asks for, and that all these things he loves shall not slip away from him, he sees that all this love of beauty and variety can only find its completion in a world where time and change have become something else than he now knows them to be. In the world of eternity then, he believes, the love of beauty is not treacherous, the romantic love of the unattainable shall be resolved in Christian terms, the unattainable shall be attained and desire shall find rest.

Then gin I thinke on that which Nature sayd,
Of that same time when no more *Change* shall be,
But stedfast rest of all things firmely stayed
Vpon the pillours of Eternity,
That is contrayr to *Mutabilitie*:
For, all that moueth, doth in *Change* delight:
But thence-forth all shall rest eternally
With Him that is the God of Sabbaoth hight:
O that great Sabbaoth God, graunt me that Sabaoths sight.
(VII. viii. 2)

When we read these words and also remember the sweep and movement of all that has gone before, the innumerable quests, the wanderings of parted lovers, the play of magic, we naturally relate that world of constant change and the love of it to the Christian satisfaction that is being affirmed here. And if the thought of this fragment can find any consistence with the rest, it would be in the transformation of the love of the far-away and the note of yearning into such a joy as Galahad's who in the attainment of his quest could finally pray that in the very joy that he then knew in the moment of mystical illumination he might move from earthly life to the celestial.

In the six books of *The Faerie Queene* none of Spenser's knights reached such joy, not even when one came to the House of Contemplation and desired to stay there. And from the way it is all presented it is clear that Spenser was not intent on such completion instantly, for them or in his own controlling of the poem. There was always Arlo-Hill, Arcadia, some other place of innocence and perfection on earth that even the gods delighted in, an innocence in life complete and apart from holiness. And there was something in the nature of love, an excellence in changing mortal life not to be renounced, not, perhaps, even to be transmuted, a perfection in a loving nature however destined to be betrayed by decay and death.

So once more one may return to consider the variety of the poem for what that can tell us about the conception of the poem, and to discover what consistency of ideas and meaning would support the power of the *Mutabilitie* cantos.

The story all began with a certain knight, like any other except that he happened to be called on to defend a maiden who sometimes requires what is needed of a defender of the truth. He is adventurous, rash, promising, not very wise, not the strongest or most skilful warrior, and initially not even a faithful lover. He is merely an ordinary knight to whom things happen. Life in the forest catches him up and nearly destroys him, at least it makes a fool of him, but in some mysterious way he is eventually led into the discipline of contemplation, and his religion is there strengthened to a holy righteousness so that he is able ultimately to defeat the great enemy who has been holding the maiden's parents captive.

Before such an ending to his journeys we have been treated to a succession of extraordinary scenes, some in which he plays no part, some that have no bearing upon his success or failure, but whether they do or not, the whole achieving effects that enrich our knowledge of the multitude of life. The effect has almost never been to increase suspense in the narrative of the knight's adventures, but it works more to increase our knowledge of the intricacy and the enigma in which any man moves. Pictures of extraordinary beauty give way to horror, just as a beautiful woman is seen suddenly to be all corruption underneath her false appearance; a magician whose wickedness terrifies us sends a spirit below the earth to the home of Morpheus, where some mysterious beauty in the sound of the water-fall nourishes his sleep; a fierce beast is suddenly a most respectful lion; a herd of satyrs are tender and most perfectly friendly—in short, this is the world of the playful imagination. The sequence of scenes and of characters is partly for the pleasure and interest of contrast, and partly for the sake of the details themselves:

> A trickling streame from high rocke tumbling downe
> And euer-drizling raine vpon the loft,
> Mixt with a murmuring winde, much like the sowne
> Of swarming Bees, did cast him in a swowne:
> No other noyse, nor peoples troublous cryes,
> As still are wont t'annoy the walled towne,
> Might there be heard: but careless Quiet lyes,
> Wrapt in eternall silence farre from enemyes.
>
> (I. i. 41)

But something else also makes itself felt as belonging to the substance of this variety, that an extraordinary number of the wanderers in the forest are lovers, parted, or searching for those they have not yet met, sometimes happily or sometimes unhappily together. Saint George is divided from Una and takes up with the false Duessa. Sans Foy and Duessa join and part, as do Duessa and Orgoglio. Two lovers live together in all but eternal misery, turned to trees. Arthur follows the dream of Glorianne. There is pair after pair, search after search, here and in all the following books, and sometimes such themes are more dominant than at others. The passiveness of the second book, on Temperance, emphasizes such stories, but what has often been called the theme of the third book might not unfairly be spoken of as the substance of them all and the explanation of the complexity of the structure:

> Wonder it is to see, in diuerse minds,
> How diuersly loue doth his pageants play.
> (III. v. 1)

There are, of course, continuously emphasized all those matters concerning the love of glory and righteousness and the love of God and of truth, but the great variety of the six books looked at together is chiefly developed in the presentation of a world of all kinds of lovers, with all the variety of their trials.

And this, it appears, is because *The Faerie Queene* begins with Ariosto. That writer meant his poem to be just that, a story of all the follies of man and especially of love, the greatest. There was nothing he would leave out, but for his purposes there was a different binding conception than Spenser would accept to provide the poem's inspiration and unity, the conception of the madness of Orlando. Spenser rejects the idea of the necessary madness of love and is taken up instead with something one must speak of as innocence, as if the love of mortals and of God might be joined, as if it were one, and in its constancy one also with the love of justice, though in this last idea he is less clear.

It is by the grace of Ariosto and in another way of Tasso that Spenser begins, moving into the romantic scene of all the traditions available to him, but as a modern beginning with Ariosto rather than Chaucer or Malory, aspiring in that lyrical meditative way of his, as he once moved from the simple pastoral to the vision and the hymn, now to the great romantic epic, still for him a lyrical form and still a kind of vision or dream. He aspires to make something else of Ariosto's poem, and to justify love as Ariosto, and Tasso with his magnificent development of pastoral had not. And so he began:

> Lo I the man, whose Muse whilome did maske,
> As time her taught, in lowly Shepheards weeds,
> Am now enforst a far vnfitter taske,
> For trumpets sterne to chaunge mine Oaten reeds,

And sing of Knights and Ladies gentle deeds;
Whose prayses hauing slept in silence long,
Me, all too meane, the sacred Muse areeds
To blazon broad emongst her learned throng:
Fierce warres and faithfull loues shall moralize my song.

Le donne, i cavallier, l'arme, gli amori,
Le cortesie, l'audaci imprese io canto,
che furo al tempo che passaro i Mori
d'Africa il mare, e in Francia nocquer tanto,
seguendo l'ire, e i giovenil furori
d'Agramante lor re, che si diè vanto
di vendicar la morte di Troiano
sopra re Carlo imperator romano.

Of Dames, of Knights, of armes, of loves delight,
Of courtesies, of high attempts I speake,
Then when the *Moores* transported all their might
On *Africke* seas, the force of *France* to breake:
Incited by the youthful heate and spight
Of *Agramant* their King, that vow'd to wreake
The death of King *Trayano* (lately slaine)
Vpon the *Romane* Emperour *Charlemaine*.

If the similarity of those first lines is clear, so are the differences, one calling our attention to the poet as a figure in an imaginary world, the muses of antiquity and shepherds, and the antique world of chivalry; the other claiming merely to recall history. But if Ariosto still provides Spenser with so much it is because for all their differences, through Ariosto Spenser is keeping in touch with what is fundamentally romantic in the literature the Renaissance is re-shaping. Ariosto himself had done something quite different from Boiardo although in one way he was merely continuing the *Orlando Innamorato*. Boiardo had made one of those simple and profound changes, combining in one story material from the Charlemagne and the Arthurian literature, bringing stories of love and all that that might mean into the world of the *chansons de geste*, and bringing the stories of religious wars into the world of courtly love and the Round Table. In Ariosto's continuation of this combining of things the intellectual and the tragic scope of both traditions was extended, and a new assimilation of chivalric poetry in the tradition of the romances was magnificently established. So now there was the Emperor, the Court, the Roman Church, the Saracens, and mingled with them men like Tristan and Sir Kay and Launcelot and heroines like Guenevere and Iseult, and, what is perhaps most interesting of all, all the variety of life at such a place as Ferrara. There was more of the ordinary and more of the heroic than in Malory, and it is from this that Spenser begins. And if we can now read the Italians with the enthusiasm they have so magnificently kindled in the past, we shall be able, I think, to orient ourselves towards some closer understanding of the unity of Spenser's conception and some surer idea of the importance to his conception of the richness of detail and the variety of scene and action.[1]

[1] It is of course most dangerous to suppose one might understand how Spenser, so far removed from us in time, understood the Italians he read and imitated. The difficulty is fantastically exaggerated when we remember the shifts even in the present century of the opinions on the *Orlando Furioso*. What we know for certain is that such poems as these deeply attracted Spenser, that Tasso's Godfrey and Rinaldo seemed to him truly heroic, and that everything he took from the Italians he made his own. But to see what stirred him first is another matter. All one can do, I think, is to pay his models the respect of understanding as far as we can their own greatness, and then act in the faith that it was their greatness that attracted him. R. E. Neil Dodge, for one, emphasizes this, that Spenser, like Harington, took the *Orlando Furioso* for a poem of great seriousness, but the statement as such cannot of course carry conviction for us unless we, too, understand how that poem lays claim to seriousness. ("Spenser's Imitations from Ariosto," *Publications of the Modern Language Association*, XII [1897], 168). It is partly the intention of the present writer to make an intelligible interpretation of Spenser's obligation to the great Italian poems by emphasizing their relation to the romantic tradition and in showing also something of Spenser's place there. There can be no demonstration of proof in these matters, but something like conviction may arise from any increase in appreciation that follows.

Alice Galimberti's book is helpful to add to the English studies of Spenser's debt to Ariosto (*Edmondo Spenser, "L'Ariosto Inglese,"* Turin: Giuseppe Gambino, 1938), although the work of Anna Benedetti seems more searching (*L' "Orlando Furioso" nella Vita Intelletuale del Popolo Inglese*, Florence, 1914). A

BOIARDO

Dame legiadre e cavallier pregiati,
Che onorati la corte e gentilezza,
Tirative davanti et ascoltati
Delli antiqui baron l'alta prodezza,
Che seran sempre in terra nominati:
Tristano e Isotta dalla bionda trezza,
Genevra e Lancilotto del re Bando;
Ma sopra tutti il franco conte Orlando.
(*Orlando Innamorato*, II. viii. 2)[1]

(Gracious ladies and esteemed knights, who
are an honour to the court and to nobility
itself, come forward and listen to stories
of the mighty prowess of the ancient barons
whose names will always live upon the
earth: Tristan and Iseult of the blonde tresses,
Guenevere and Launcelot, subjects of
King Bando, and above all the Frankish
count Orlando.)[2]

Rajna observed that Boiardo could not have succeeded in joining in one poem the worlds of Arthur and Charlemagne had they not for him ceased to have a separate existence, and if for him

fine study on the influence of Tasso is Alberto Castelli's *La Gerusalemme Liberata nella Inghilterra di Spenser*, Milan: Pubblicazioni della Università Cattolica del Sacro Cuore: Serie Quarta, Scienze Filologiche, XX), 1936.

Mrs. Josephine Waters Bennett has argued that we shall gain more insight into *The Fairie Queene* by regarding Spenser as "a Protestante Dante" than "by studying his debt to Ariosto and Tasso and considering the *Faerie Queene* in the non-existent genre of 'epic-romance'." ("Genre, Milieu, and the 'Epic-Romance'," *English Institute Essays, 1951*, New York; Columbia University Press, 1952, p. 125). Questions of genre apart, Mrs. Bennett would agree, I am sure, that the Italian romance writers offer a great deal in the illumination of Spenser's writing.

[1] In *Tutte Le Opere di Matteo M. Boiardo*, ed. Angelandrea Zottoli, Milan: Mondadori, 1936 (Vol. I).

[2] The translations of Boiardo in parentheses are mine.

they had not already lost all distinctions from each other and been mingled in still another conception, the ideal of chivalry.[1] That mingling, that great innovation that was to set the style for so many to come after him, a unity of worlds Ariosto and Spenser accepted as a matter of course and as the very centre of their own greatest works, could not have been anything merely accidentally or coldly conceived. In part it might have been, as Rajna suggested, in the need Boiardo felt to rescue the Carolingian poetry from the merely vegetable life that was all that now remained in it.[2] But even such a conception would have been subordinate to the truly formative power in Boiardo, the power born of his single-mindedness, his exaltation of truth and of a way of living according to the truth. For him that was clearly chivalry, and chivalry meant loyalty, courtesy, valour, unselfishness and piety, in war and in love,[3] all supported by what Croce called his character as a writer "appassionato dell'energico."[4]

While there could hardly be more emphasis than the *Innamorato* gives to the honour gained in war, even this is subordinate to its valuing of love. This is clear in the simplest and most obvious way from the beginning in the search of Orlando for Angelica. And so many lovers come into this rambling story in such number and enthusiasm that their romantic amorousness fixes the poem's character. It is almost a matter of overweighing, for the idea of the importance of love and the charm of the stories of love are not often joined in any natural way with the stories of war and adventure. Perhaps even more significantly, ideas of the nature of love are not often related to the ideas of honour, or to the faith that is involved in the war against the infidels.

If there is no integration of such matters one may see that the poem's narrative method is part of the cause. One incident is developed, a warrior is knocked from a horse, and before we know enough to inquire curiously if he is to live or die, some other story

[1] Pio Rajna, Preface to *L'Orlando Innamorato*, Milan: La Santa, 1929, pp. 27–28.

[2] *Ibid.*, p. 30.

[3] Giulio Reichenbach, *L'Orlando Innamorato di M. M. Boiardo*, Florence: La Nuova Italia, 1936, p. 228.

[4] *Ariosto, Shakespeare, e Corneille*, Bari, 1920, p. 68.

is taken up, half-started, and then interrupted by another. Stories break off in the middle of a stanza again and again, and without the accretion of suspense that forms when Tasso does the same kind of thing.[1] It is equally without the humorous suspense of Ariosto, although he, too, is as dependent on this manner of *entrelacement*. The method of Boiardo, however, has another virtue than that relating to narrative. It expresses especially the interest of novelty, of the vitality that is always seeking for new names, new faces, new countries. Sometimes this seems close to garrulity, it is true, and the constant reminder at the beginning of so many cantos that these are stories told by a man who has gathered friends to listen to him reinforces the notion. For all that, the fact that a fierce battle can begin and end in a single stanza, by the very neglect of narrative interests keeps bringing us back to the recognition that the most serious matter has to do with love, and indeed once that is mentioned the poetry quickens and reaches for a while the strength of sustainment.

[1] E. G. Gardner remarked that Boiardo largely developed the system of *entrelacement*, a method found, of course, earlier in the *cantari* and French prose romances of the Arthurian cycle as well as in their Italian imitators. (*The Arthurian Legend in Italian Literature*, London, 1930, p. 282.) In Boiardo it goes along with his restlessness and his continuous interest in relating all the practical details of war and fighting and heroism. This point is well made in Emilio Bigi, *La Poesia del Boiardo*, Florence: Sansoni, 1941, p. 15 (Studi di Lettere, Storia e Filosofia Pubblicati dalla R. Scuola Normale Superiore di Pisa, XX). There is also a famous anecdote:

"Il créait dans la joie, peut-on dire; car, avant de prendre la plume, il vivait, par l'imagination, les aventures de ses héros; c'était son propre rêve qu'il animait, qu'il réalisait en eux. On a cité cent fois cette anecdote caractéristique: Boiardo promenait sa rêverie poétique à travers les collines, les vallées, les forêts et les plaines voisines de Scandiano, façonnant dans sa pensée la personnalité morale de ses héros, leur donnant des noms bien adaptés à leur physionomie. Le jour où, au cours de ses chevauchées, il trouva le nom de 'Rodamonte'—qui deviendra Rodomont chez l'Arioste—ce nom lui parut si sonore et si expressif qu'il le cria joyeusement à tous les échos d'un bois—qui portait lui-même un nom retentissant, 'il bosco del Fracasso'!—Rentré à Scandiano au galop de sa monture, il fit sonner les cloches des églises pour fêter le baptême de ce héros chimérique, qui a fourni, on doit l'avouer, une assez belle carrière parmi les personnages de romans!" (Henri Hauvette, *L'Arioste et la Poésie Chevaleresque à Ferrare au Début du XVIe Siècle*, 2nd edition, Paris, 1927, pp. 64–65).

Despite the almost heedlessness of some elementary matters of narrative method Boiardo introduced several of the very best of romantic episodes, of a kind Spenser could not resist although for some reason or other they were less attractive to Ariosto. The very first event of any consequence in the poem is one of these—suddenly there appears in the midst of Charlemagne's court, no one knows how, a damsel and a cavalier, followed by four giants (I. i. 21). Just that. And there are many other similar wonders: a ship furnished with all luxuries, food and wine, yet managed without hands (I. v. 55); a serpent that breathes fire and poison (I. xxvi. 29); a slain giant whose blood, as it pours over the ground, turns to flame, and from this first one then another giant takes form (II. iv. 74); a plant to be climbed like Jack's Beantsalk (II. v. 4);[1] a book whose lettering was all in blood (I. xiii. 29); a serpent changed into a woman (II. xxvi. 14). Some details, it is true, are ornate to the last touch of extravagance, and are frigid or ridiculous:

> Io vengo a ricontarvi in questo giorno
> La piu fiera battaglia é sterminata,
> E la più orrenda e più pericolosa
> Che racontasse mai verso né prosa.
>
> (II. xxx. 1)
>
> (I come to tell you today of the most
> fierce and endless battle, and the most
> horrifying and dangerous that verse
> or prose ever related.)

> E sì forte battea dente con dente,
> Che di lontan il gran romor se odiva.
>
> (I. xxvi. 29)
>
> (And the teeth scraped against each
> other so hard the great noise could be
> heard far off.)

[1] Ferdinando Neri has written perceptively although briefly of Boiardo's use of material from folk-lore in *Storia e Poesia*, Turin: Chiantore, 1944, pp. 37–41.

Some have the authentic folklore extravagance, others the sophistication of romances that have become tawdry; and if there is humour, as often enough, it is for its own sake and not to mock romances or chivalry:

> Ben cento pedi quel balcone era alto:
> Se la vecchia se occise, io nol domando.
>
> (I. ix. 35)
>
> (That balcony was a good hundred feet
> high; if the old one kills herself I'll
> make no inquiries.)

> Tira Dudone adosso a quel malvaso,
> Sopra il frontale ad ambe mani il tocca;
> Roppe ad un colpo tutto quanto il naso,
> E ben tre denti li cacciò di bocca.
> Senza sapone il mento gli ebbe raso.
>
> (II. x. 19)
>
> (Dudone approached that ill-looking
> one from the back, and put both his
> hands over his face. With one crack
> he broke his nose to bits and
> drove three teeth out of his mouth.
> Without soap he shaved his chin.)

The extravagances never lead to the mockery of greatness, not even of that fantastically great hero Gradasso:

> Settanta dui reami in sua possanza
> Ha conquistato con la sua persona.
>
> (II. v. 56)
>
> (In his own person he had taken
> possession of seventy-two kingdoms.)

Nor is there mockery in the multiplication of wonders:

> Due dame ritrovarno con duo nani.
>
> (III. ii. 40)
>
> (Two ladies accompanied by two dwarves.)

And when the cruelty and the blood-letting pass bounds that should call for some comment, in humour or denunciation, there is none, and the extravagance of the fact is allowed to bring no discredit upon the life of chivalry and war:

> Io presi per li piedi quel meschino,
> E detti il capo a un sasso prossimano.
> Te par ch'io vendicassi il mio dispetto?
> Ma questo fu un principio, e non lo effetto.
>
> Quasi vivendo ancora lo squartai;
> De il petto a l'luno e a l'altro trassi il core.
> Le piccolette membra minuzzai:
> Pensa se, ciò facendo, avia dolore!
>
> (I. viii. 39–40)
>
> (I grabbed that rascal by his feet and
> gave his head to a neighbouring rock.
> Do you think I avenged my insult?
> But this was the beginning and not the end.
>
> Still half living I quartered him, I drew his
> heart out of his breast little by little, I
> broke the little members into small pieces.
> Imagine how that hurt!)

But whatever might have happened to the narrative in other hands, and however much interested Boiardo himself is in his Charlemagne material and the folklore that is part of it, the love and chivalry of the romances attract and hold his greatest interest. Faithful always to the form of the Charlemagne matter, as Ariosto after him, and as Spenser was not, in fact rescuing some of its stories from the degeneration one observes even in *I Reali di Francia* and in *The Four Sons of Aymon*, where the activities and ethics of the central characters are those of young hoodlums, Boiardo's humanism and his love of love add some more noble interest to his poem.

Perhaps the finest statement of the importance of love to him begins with these lines:

Luce de gli occhi miei, spirto del core,
Per cui cantar suolea sì dolcemente
Rime legiadre e bei versi d'amore,
Spirami aiuto alla istoria presente.
Tu sola al canto mio facesti onore,
Quando di te parlai primeramente,
Perché a qualunche che di te ragiona,
Amor la voce e l'intelletto dona.

(II. iv. 1)

(Light of my eyes, breath of my heart, by
whose grace I am wont to sing so sweetly
delightful rhymes and beautiful verses of
love, inspire me now to tell this story.
Thou alone didst honour to my singing when I
first spoke of thee, for Love endows the voice
and mind of whoever reasons of thee.)

His confidence at times is complete—at least if Tisbina's sentiments are his:

Deh quanta è paccia quella alma che crede
Che Amor non possa ogni cosa compire!

(I. xii. 45)

(What a stupid soul who should believe that
Love cannot accomplish everything!)

Although one can hardly be sure how much he means this, he affirms that the power of love is not limited to the gentle, for it rules:

La bassa plebe col segnore altiero.

(I. xxviii. 2)

(The lowly plebs along with the lofty lord.)

There are, furthermore, extravagances of statement he allows himself that go to the extreme that we expect to find only in inferior writing, and that do not seem quite consonant with Boiardo's general nature. For example, in the strange story of Prasildo and Tisbina, when in a plot to deceive him Tisbina foolishly says,

> E mia persona ti darò per merto
> Di tal servigio: tientine ben certo,
> (I. xii. 28)

> (As a reward for such a service I shall give
> thee my person, be sure of that,)

she is unexpectedly obliged to make the promise good. Meanwhile, her lover has killed himself and so faced by a double catastrophe she says as to the dead man:

> Per mantenirte quel che te ho giurato,
> Perdo la vita, et ho perso l'onore;
> Ma, quel ch'è più, colui che tanto ho amato
> Perdo con seco, e lascio questo mondo.
> (I. xii. 65)

> (In order to keep my oath to thee I am losing
> my life as I have already lost my honour; but
> what is more, I lose with thee the one I have
> so much loved; and so I leave this world.)

The comparison is nearly as extravagant as Dryden's

> 'Twas heav'n, or somewhat more.

And if statements of this kind are rare in Boiardo, the sentiment is nevertheless implicit in the degree of indignity to which love can reduce its victims. There is, for example, the picture of Orlando at the beginning of the poem, Orlando the great warrior—

E sopra al letto suo cadde invilito,
Tanto è il dolor che dentro lo martella—
(I. ii. 22)

This valiant Knight, true Valors chiefest Ioy,
Weepes on his Pallet like a peeuish Boy[1]—

speaking of himself,

Et io, come dolente feminella,
Tengo la guancia posata alla mano,
E sol me aiuto lacrimando in vano.
(I. ii. 25)

The whilst like to a puling woman I,
Leane with my hand vppon my face with griefe,
Easing my selfe with tears without reliefe.
(Sig. E_3)

Angelica, too, is similarly carried away:

E dove giacque Ranaldo sereno,
Bacia quelle erbe e di pianger se appaga.
(I. iii. 50)

And for to kisse those flowers shee takes delight,
Which by the place where *Rinald* lay she found.
(Sig. H_3)

The boasting that such love occasions is outrageous:

E' mi dà il core,
Senza elmo, senza maglia e senza scudo,
Aver con teco di guerra l'onore;
Così mi vanto di combatter nudo
Per aquistare il desiato amore.—

1 *Orlando Innamorato, The three first Bookes . . . Done into English Heroicall Verse*, by Robert Tofte, London, 1598, Sig. E_2v. It is actually only the first three cantos of the first book that are here translated: I have used Tofte's translation for the passages I cite from these cantos.

Cotal parole usava il baron drudo,
Però ch'Amor l'avea posto in tal loco,
Che per colei s'arìa gettato in foco.
(I. i 86)

and yet my minde me tels,
Withouten helmet, armour or with sword,
I shall thee conquer, though I nought haue els,
Naked with thee to fight I can afford
For my deere Love (despite of charming Spels:)
Thus braude this Baron, not one foote thence sturd:
For Love had him so heated with desire,
He would for her haue lept into the fire.
(Sig. D_2)

But perhaps the greatest extravagance is from the Arthurian matter itself:

E qual fia quel che, odendo de Tristano
E de sua dama ciò che se ne dice,
Che non mova ad amarli il cor umano,
Reputando il suo fin dolce e felice,
Che, viso a viso essendo e mano a mano
E il cor col cor più stretto alla radice,
Ne le braccia l'un l'altro a tal conforto
Ciascun di lor rimase a un ponto morto?
(II. xxvi. 2)

(And what sort of person would that be who, hearing what they tell of Tristan and his lady would not be moved to love the human heart, seeing how sweet and happy their end, face to face and hand in hand, and heart bound tightly to heart at the very roots, in each other's arms taking such joy that each died in the same instant?)

These exaggerations testify, I think, to the inability of Boiardo to combine perfectly the unity of the chivalric life as conceived in the stories around Charlemagne with the central conceptions of the Arthurian legend. There should be for real unity a way of presenting the champion of Christendom as also a kind of melancholy Tristan,[1] but the disjointedness in this poem is obviously evident in the constant association of stories of love with scenes of pastoral peace, for Boiardo, whatever his passion for chivalry, could not finally reconcile the claims of war and love. The failure is particularly clear when the contrast is made with Ariosto whose protests against war were so deep, but who in his praise of love found no need to provide the conditions of pastoral peace to guarantee its success.

In Boiardo the world is at its best—

> Nel grazïoso tempo onde natura
> Fa più lucente la stella d'amore,
> Quando la terra copre di verdura,
> E li arboscelli adorna di bel fiore,
> Giovani e dame et ogni creatura
> Fanno allegrezza con zoioso core;
> Ma poi che 'l verno viene e il tempo passa,
> Fugge il diletto e quel piacer si lassa.
>
> (II. i. 1)

> (In the gracious time when nature causes the star of love to shine most brightly, when she covers the earth with green and adorns the small trees with flowers, she makes youths and ladies and every creature happy and joyous in heart. But when winter comes and the season changes, delight runs away and all that pleasure is left behind.)

In the antique world even war was in the service of love:

> Così nel tempo che virtù fioria
> Ne li antiqui segnori e cavallieri
> Con noi stava allegrezza e cortesia,
> E poi fuggirno per strani sentieri,

[1] Francesco Foffano writes perceptively on this matter in "I Precursori del Bojardo," extracted from *Rivista d'Italia*, VIII (1905).

Sì che un gran tempo smarirno la via,
Né del più ritornar ferno pensieri;
Ora è il mal vento e quel verno compito,
E torna il mondo di virtù fiorito.

Et io cantando torno alla memoria
Delle prodezze de' tempi passati,
E contarovi la più bella istoria
(Se con quïete attenti me ascoltati)
Che fusse mai nel mondo, e di più gloria,
Dove odireti e degni atti e pregiati
De' cavallier antiqui, e le contese
Che fece Orlando alor che amor il prese.

(II. i. 2–3)

(So it was once when virtue flowered in the ancient lords and knights, and joy and courtesy reigned among us, but there came a time when these left us by strange paths. A great storm confused our road, and the thought of ever returning was put aside. Now the ill wind and winter is over, and the world is again flowering in virtue.

And in my singing I return to the memory of the prowess of times past, and I shall tell you the finest story [if you listen to me quietly] that there ever was in the world, and of the greatest glory, and you shall hear the most worthy and honoured deeds of ancient knights, and the fights of Orlando when love took hold of him.)

Away from war—

E un ruscelletto di fontana viva
Mormorando passava per quel prato.
Brandimarte, che stava in quella riva,
Per molto affanno in quel giorno durato,
Nel bel pensar de amor qui se adormiva.

(I. xix. 64)

(A small stream from a living fountain passed
murmuring through that meadow. When Brandimarte
came to its bank, he fell asleep there, tired
from the labour of the day, and he slept in the
gracious thought of love.)

Even in such a scene there is the failure to harmonize the ideas of peace and love and chivalry, a harmony Spenser was more successful in achieving. Still one ought not to say that Boiardo failed at all points:

Quando la terra più verde è fiorita,
E più sereno il cielo e grazïoso,
Alor cantando il rosignol se aita
La notte e il giorno a l'arboscello ombroso;
Così lieta stagione ora me invita
A seguitare il canto dilettoso,
E racontare il pregio e 'l grand'onore
Che donan l'arme gionte con amore.
(II. viii. 1)

(When the most green earth is covered with
flowers and the sky is most bright and lovely,
then the nightingale by his singing rejoices
night and day in a shady bush, even so the
joyful season invites me now to pursue the
delightful song, and tell of the reward and
the high honour that arms win when they are
joined with love.)

It may be that the allegory of the poem represents an effort at further, more comprehensive unification of the poem's matter, with the intention of philosophical coherence. It is true that allegory is more congenial to Boiardo than to Ariosto, and despite the often archaic, medieval suggestions is more nearly comparable to Spenser's method. The advanced manner of allegory where there is so much delight in the simple visualizing is perhaps the comparison one needs to make in reading the descriptions of the three Graces and the God of Love in the scene where Ranaldo is overcome and bound with flowers (II. xv. 43–62). Something of the formal, almost stiffly conventional style of allegorizing characterizes the scene where Prasildo goes to the Garden of Medusa on a mission, entering by the Gate of Poverty (I. xii. 26 ff.), but even this is less contrived for the sake of significance than the comparable kind of incident in Spenser. And there is another kind of allegory with symbolic more than allegorical charm: Orlando comes into a magic garden and a palace, he passes a dragon, and everywhere in the scene there is the sense of the mysteriousness of beauty, and such an emphasis on sensation as it is not in the nature of allegory to tolerate (II. iv). But none of these has the dramatic power of the passage on Discord in Ariosto (XXVI–XXVII), and none of these differing methods seems to be part of the conception of the whole although they may witness the hope of unity.

There is in Boiardo as in Spenser a simplicity, a singleness of purpose, a repetitiousness even, the repetitiousness that belongs to the committed, something one does not find in Ariosto, and that makes it useful to compare Boiardo's poem with Spenser's whatever the particular obligations may be.[1] It is a kind of simplicity accompanied by a disposition to wonder no longer possible apparently to Ariosto, who is so much more tragically perceptive. And if Ariosto's poem is the one Spenser starts from there are at least these harmonies with Boiardo and these *naïvetés* of technique which represent part of what Spenser will bring to all else he offers in going on from Ariosto.

There is much less of the air of greatness in Boiardo than in Spenser, the allegory is scantier, the language is often coarse, and there is curiously less of the lyrical, in the parts or in the whole tone. But the marks of intimacy in Boiardo are much more in Spenser's manner than anything in any other of the great Italians —the small prefaces calling attention to the poet himself, the nostalgia and the praise of the past, the continuation of

[1] A few indications of such indebtedness are assembled in the Variorum *Spenser*, II, 444.

genealogies of the patrons of the poem into prophecies for the future restoration of peace and for the return of Astraea. It is the courage of Boiardo's simplicity that persists in Spenser in the midst of all the other richness.

ARIOSTO

To a reader brought up chiefly on English literature the *Orlando Furioso* must appear a Catholic poem, a great spectacle about birth and death and marriage, full of ceremony and the splendour of an imperial line obedient to the Roman Church. The faithful war against the unfaithful, prayers are offered, conversions sought for, God and Christ and the Angels take part in the poem in their mysterious ways. The poem approaches its end with a funeral procession, there is an oration calling to mind the authority of both Empire and Church,[1] and a splendid ceremony, and not long after that there is a marriage which is in more than one way the central motive of the poem, a marriage of a Christian and a Catholic kind.[2] And the poem is also a romance, a poem of

1 "Il resto dell'orazione è la parte, diremo così, ufficiale, obbligatoria, è la voce del massimo rappresentante dell'Impero e della Cristianità romana in quella pompa funebre, non è voce del lirismo d'Orlando, eroe di vita intima appassionata che il dolore nutre e distrugge." (Giuseppina Fumagalli, *Unità Fantastica dell'Orlando Furioso*, Milan: Giuseppe Principato, n. d., p. 65.)

2 There are different ways in which the marriage may be regarded as the central subject of the poem. Pigna's early analysis, arguing for the reading of the poem as one devoted to the praise of the Este family, poi[illegible] to Ruggiero as the original of that stock: "Ma perche su colui, che da noi è [illegible]o, finir bisogna; essendo che condotto lui oue vogliamo, piu altro non [illegible]mane; in Ruggero debitamente questo Furioso [the poem] si va à risoluere. & perche tra tutte l'imprese di Ruggero vna vi è su che si fonda il poeta piu che sopra alcuna altra; & perche questa tale è il conquistar Brandamante; perciò hauuta ch'egli l'hebbe il tutto era conchiuso: se non che quietamente hauerla non potea, se prima la querela, ch' era tra Rodamonte & lui, decisa non era. & cosi vcciso che è Rodamonte, altro piu non ha da venire: & altro medesimamente da venire non ha, per esser giunto Ruggero à tal impresa che ad vna maggiore arriuar non potea. Ma pigliata è questa attione circa il prender Brandamante per moglie: essendo che da questo congiungimento la stirpe da Este ne segue, per cui egli à scriuere si mosse." (*I Romanzi Di M. Giouan Battista Pigna, Al S. Donno Luigi Da Este Vescovo Di Ferrara, Divisa In Tre Libri. Ne quali della Poesia, & della vita dell' Ariosto con nuouo modo si tratta.* Venice: Valgrisi, 1554, pp. 78–79.)

A recent writer, without reference to the Este's, affirms the importance of the

fantastic adventures, the marvellous its very atmosphere,[1] the mysterious exploited from the beginning:

> Sei giorni me n'andai matina e sera
> per balze e per pendici orride e strane,
> dove non via, dove sentier non era,
> dove né segno di vestigie umane.
>
> (II. xli)

> A senight space abating but a day,
> About the woods and mountaines I did range,
> In savage deserts wilde and void of way,
> Where humane steps were rare and very strange.

The variousness of the poem permits some of the extremes of the romance material their chance and a beauty in exaggeration that I think Spenser did not attempt. One sees this in the incident of the knight who has come to defend Ginevra, not knowing whether she is guilty of unfaithfulness or not. He is brought to see her treachery with his own eyes, and yet he trusts his love for her so much he is persuaded that what he has just seen is not true:

> Ella è pur la mia donna e la mia dea,
> questa è la luce pur degli occhi miei:
> convien ch'a dritto e a torto, per suo scampo
> pigli l'impresa, e resti morto in campo.
>
> (VI. x)

marriage plot over that in which the story of Orlando is related. "Il motivo centrale, nel quale si riassumono le mille diverse voci del *Furioso*, è costituito dalle nozze di Ruggiero. Neppure la pazzia di Orlando, che pure dà il titolo al libro, riesce ad ugagliare quel motivo nè a vincere l'insistenza, la profondità e—sopra tutto—la continuità." (Ezio Levi, "L' 'Orlando furioso' come epopea nuziale," *Archivum Romanicum*, XVII [1934], 459.)

Carducci had earlier commented on the way in which Ariosto, first following Boiardo's kind of narrative, had shortly begun to give Ruggiero and Bradamante dominance over all the others, in the end "facendo del loro matrimonio il soggetto principale del poema." ("Su l'Orlando Furioso," in *Edizione Nazionale delle Opere di Giosue Carducci*, XIV [Bologna, 1944], p. 92.)

[1] For interesting comment on this factor one may refer to Attilio Momigliano, *Saggio su l'* "Orlando Furioso," 3rd ed., Bari: Laterza, 1946, p. 51.

She is my saint, in her my blisse doth bide,
Her golden rayes my eies light still maintaine,
Fall backe, fall edge, and be it wrong or right,
In her defence I am resolv'd to fight.

And everywhere in the telling of wonders and of the intertwined quests of innumerable lovers and seekers after honour, for all the comedy and wit and the occasional sereneness there is the everlasting note of yearning:

come, poi che la luce è dipartita,
riman tra' boschi la smarrita agnella,
che dal pastor sperando essere udita,
si va lagnando in questa parte e in quella;
tanto che 'l lupo l'ode da lontano,
e 'l misero pastor ne piagne invano.[1]
(VIII. lxxvi)

Even like a lambe when starres do first appeare,
(Her dame and shepheard being out of vew)
Bleateth aloud to make the shepheard heare,
And in her kind her evill hap doth rew,
Vntill the wolfe doth find her to her paine,
The silly shepheard seeking her in vaine.
(VIII. 67)

To the end the great work remains a romance despite the immediacy that comes into the expression of passion at many places. It does not take on the greatest epic sound if one may signify by that a celebration of greatness undiminished by the sense of a glory

[1] "Sei versi. Circola in essi una larga e mestissima armonia che apre spazi e silenzi notturni di campi, in cui erra solo il debole belato; l'odono da lontananze remote due esseri. Ben disformi. Il giorno è spento, e il dramma che si compie nella campagna deserta e che il pastore (Orlando) vive fantasticamente fino a piangerne, è ricco d'effetti patetici: desolazione della pecora spersa che invoca inutilmente aiuto, ferocia del lupo che avanza da chi sa quale fosca tana all' incauto richiamo, ricerca ansiosa, disperazione vana del pastore impotente a salvarla." (Fumagalli, *Unità Fantastica dell'Orlando Furioso*, p. 9.)

that has vanished from the earth. Although from time to time one or another hero takes on enormous qualities—Orlando most notably, but also Rinaldo and Ruggiero and Bradamante—none ever meets an enemy of the greatest quality, of the quality of Hector or Satan or even of Godfrey, nor indeed ever meets man or fortune with the resources of the fullest human capacity. However fierce the combat it will always turn out that some weapon is enchanted, or some magician willl intervene, and never does mere humanity measure itself against the full weight of the world or the enmity of the gods.

And for all the poem's loyalty to Catholicism there lacks the feeling of the sacredness of a cause, and there is nothing like that patriotism that is so important a factor in the greatness of the *Chanson de Roland* and that gives the *Aeneid* so much of its weight, no granting of sacred authority to the claims of nationality so that the struggles for honour and love and truth the poem tells about might involve the strength of such divine commitments. And curiously, even in the conflicts of Saracens and Christians there is not the intensity of partisan feeling that comes into Spenser's stories about the English in Ireland, to say nothing of the fervour of the religiousness urging the crusaders of the *Gerusalemme Liberata.*[1]

And as a poem full of ceremony and romance it is still something else, and this is its most stirring interest, a poem about the intricate movement of life, the great rush in which men and women are driven, in which they meet and part, hoping always for the rest they think they can find only in love and human faithfulness.[2] Everything leads to marriage and everything parts

[1] "On chercherait vainement, dans le Roland Furieux, une pensée politique présentant quelque unité. . . ." (Hauvette, *L'Arioste et la Poésie Chevaleresque à Ferrare au Début du XVI*[e] *Siècle*, p. 264.)

[2] Momigliano's comment on this aspect of the poem is notable: "L'opera suprema dell'Ariosto è dare una veste affascinante al Caso che move tutto il poema: fare dell'*Orlando* una cangiante fantasmagoria, una rete di strade innumerevoli, dove il lettore non si smarrisce e non si stanca perchè il volo del poeta è sempre accompagnato dalla beatitudine del suo pellegrinare." (*Saggio su l' "Orlando Furioso,"* p. 4.)

This may also be what one critic means when he speaks of "Questa poesia

the lovers, war, the conflicts of honour, and the claims of kin—the mere loom of life, *la gran tela* (XIII. lxxxi). It is through this that the poem develops its tragic feeling.

The most significant and most perfect incident in this regard is the final dilemma of Ruggiero. Although Bradamante is promised to him, he believes her parents will take her away and give her to the son of the Emperor of the East. There is nothing he can do—her parents must be obeyed, and he is poor. He goes away, and then it occurs to him that he can win Bradamante after all if he can find this man who is supposed to have her and if he can kill him. It is as simple as that. The fight would be honourably fought, and the rival would be removed. But an unimaginable misadventure foils him. In the enemy's territory he is taken prisoner one night when he is asleep, and he would have been slain if the man he had come to kill had not interceded for him. That same man, not knowing that this is Ruggiero, calls upon him to repay his obligation by fighting in his behalf in a joust, where, as it turns out, the victory of Ruggiero would hand over Bradamante to the very rival he has come to kill. The fantastic irony does not rest there, when he fulfils his obligation to the man who has saved his life. For the opponent in the joust is Bradamante herself and she has set the terms of the conflict, gaining from Charlemagne the promise that she shall be given in marriage to no one but that warrior who shall be able to withstand her in single combat lasting from dawn to dusk. And Ruggiero, owing all he does to the Eastern prince, cannot refuse to represent him, and in honour cannot allow himself to be defeated.

del moto" (Giuseppe Raniòlo, *Lo Spirito e l'Arte dell'Orlando Furioso*, Milan, 1929, p. 50); perhaps what Momigliano means in another way—"Questa perenne mobilità luminosa e musicale è la caratteristica che distingue questo da tutti gli altri scrittori italiani" ("La realtà e il sogno nell' 'Orlando Furioso'," *Giornale Storico della Letteratura Italiana*, LXXXV (1925), 282). But the most delightful characterization of this quality is the anecdote told of Foscolo: ". . . un giorno, mostrando dal molo di Dunkerque le lunghe onde le quali l'Oceano rompea sulla spiaggia, esclamò: così vien poetando l'Ariosto!" (Quoted by Walter Binni, *Metodo e Poesia di Ludovico Ariosto*, Messina: G. D'Anna, 1947, pp. 74–75.)

The intricacy of the entire poem is of this kind, not only an ironic but a majestic copy of all those confusions that part lovers. The intricacy, the coherence of the vast confusion is the poem, created in the single need to find a constancy in human love that can resist the furious mechanics of the world. One may suppose that it is this that Spenser sympathized with immediately. And the climax of the *Furioso* with what follows gives the sorrowful conception its most poignant sound.

There is, first, the funeral of Gradasso, all the splendour and human glory that can be attached to so great a death, and celebrations with lights and bright colours, and then the rulers of the world in procession. Shortly afterwards there is a marriage, the natural hopefulness of life is seen to follow the bitterest of trials, all happiness and gallant pleasure and sunlight and feasting, until an interruption comes to give the last sharp note to the poem. Some raving warrior has come to fight the groom, and there is the fight right then, knees in the stomach, fingers at the throat, nails in the eyes, and death. These in the very last lines, with the announcement that this is but another beginning, for there are still other wars now in the East, there are kingdoms yet to be won, and once more wives must be left behind.

It is this complexity, this fullness of truth that makes the great variety of the poem necessary. And for all the drift of the poem, the sense of rush, happinesses interrupted, and the terrible overshadowing of perpetual war, no nostalgia comes into it for days of peace in some golden age. The comic smile gets its full play instead, and it lends its strength to the poem and it is never qualified by pastoral melancholy. It is rather curious to find a poem in the Renaissance that is in many ways true to the fundamental conceptions of romances and succeeding so thoroughly in avoiding the pastoral, a poem so given to the praise of love yet free from the thought of a golden age in the past. It is true that from time to time there is a comment on the degeneration of manners in the poet's time (although more than matched by the particular felicities of the Estes' rule in Ferrara), and sometimes there is a reference to the beauty we ordinarily expect to find only in the pastoral world—

Vaghi boschetti di soavi allori,
di palme e d'amenissime mortelle,
cedri et aranci ch'avean frutti e fiori
contesti in varie forme e tutte belle,
facean riparo ai fervidi calori
de' gïorni estivi con lor spesse ombrelle;
e tra quei rami con sicuri voli
cantando se ne gíano i rosignuoli.

(VI. xxi)

Heere divers groves there were, of dainty shade,
Of Palme, or Orenge trees, of Cedars tall,
Of sundrie fruites and flowers that never fade,
The shew was faire, the plenty was not small.
And arbours in the thickest places made,
Where little light and heat came not at all:
Where Nightingales did straine their little throtes,
Recording still their sweete and pleasant notes.

Once there is a visit to an Earthly Paradise (XXXIV. xlviii), but whenever there comes a sight of some such beauty the comical is also soon to appear, lest we should forget reality—

dormeno intanto i pesci in mar quïeti
(XL. xlv)

The while the fish in sea do quiet lye.
(XL. 42)

If, on one account, the pastoral emotions are not allowed to remove or qualify the tragic bitterness, on another they are neglected because in this poem the intellect will never bow to any but the most serious allurements and because the poet insists above all else on writing about the present. The pastoral cannot belong to a conception that depends on a technique (so different from Spenser's) where each story is told as if the poet had been present, a witness remembering, for example, that such an event took place—

Tra il fin d'ottobre e il capo di novembre.
(IX. vii)

[Between the end of October and the beginning
of November.]

Ariosto tells his stories as if he had been at the shoulder of each warrior in the scene, and with his circumstantiality he achieves his special authority over us:

Strepito ascolta e spaventol suono
d'arme percosse insieme; onde s'affretta
tra pianta e pianta.
(XI. xvi)

It seem'd the wood adjoyn'd some sound did yield,
And still the neare and nearer that he goes,
The plainer sound he heard of sturdy bloes.
(XI. 14)

So immediate to him are the experiences he describes and so direct is his method, that he can say, without any loss to the fiction itself,

Gravi pene in amor si provan molte,
di che patito io n'ho la maggior parte.
(XVI. i)

Great paines in love full many men have found,
Of which my self have prov'd so great a part.

And there is no place for nostalgia here to capture the poem because Ariosto wants us to know and never to forget that at any moment, anywhere, any character might slip into hell—given so to love, might indeed expect to—

Di ciò, cor mio, nessun timor vi tocchi;
ch'io vo' seguirvi o in cielo o ne lo 'nferno.
(XXIV. lxxxi)

[Have no fear of that, my love, for I shall follow
thee whether it be in Heaven or in Hell.]

come a colei che piú che gli occhi sui,
piú che 'l suo cor, piú che la propria vita
Ruggiero amò. . . .

(IV. xli)

[As one who loved Ruggiero more than her eyes,
her heart, her life itself.]

che non è in somma amor, se non insania,
a giudizio de' savi universale.

(XXIV. i)

And madness meer, in love to overshoot,
The fool hath felt, the wise hath ever taught.

né lo posso frenar, che non ha freno.

(XXXII. xxii)

[I cannot rein (my love) for I have no rein.]

Varii gli effetti son, ma la pazzia
è tutt'una però, che li fa uscire.
Gli è come una gran selva, ove la via
conviene a forza, a chi vi va, fallire:
chi su, chi giú, chi qua, chi lá travia.
Per concludere in somma, io vi vo' dire:
a chi in amor s'invecchia, oltr'ogni pena,
si convengono i ceppi e la catena.

(XXIV. ii)

Now though effects prove not in all alike,
Yet all are mad in sort, all go astray,
As in a wildernesse where men do seek,
And more and more in seeking lose their way,
Wherefore let no man this my wish mislike,
In whom fond love shall carie long the sway,
I wish for dew reward such dolting dolts,
Like wilfull prisners, store of iron bolts.

And love is always turning into unfaithfulness, or into the

appearance of it, bringing such misery that of almost anyone it might be said,

> né men d'un vero sasso, un sasso pare.
> (X. xxxiv)
>
> And seemes as senslesse as the senslesse stone.
> (X. 32)

> Le donne, che si videro tradite
> dai loro amanti in che piú fede aveano,
> restâr per alcun dí sí sbigotite,
> che statue immote in lito al mar pareano.
> (XX. xxii)
>
> Sore were the damsels daunted and dismaid,
> When once they saw their loves had them foresaken,
> For what more spite can be, then be betraid
> Of him to whom one hath her selfe betaken?
> (XX. 21)

And "l'amorosa inchiesta" (IX. vii) always comes to

> le fatiche e gli affanni che sostenne
> nel gran disio, di che a fin mai non venne.
> (XII. lxvi)
>
> such travell and such paine,
> Nor time it selfe, that sorrowes doth appease,
> Could grant to this his griefe an end or ease.
> (XII. 51)

The wit of the poet, the free comment on the troubles of love, could hardly permit any emphasis on *la prima etá de l'oro* (III. xviii), but more than that, the sense of tragedy is too close. It is as ready to break into the poem as the humour, for Ariosto remembers anguish too well in all those circumstances that interfere with love, and especially in the hell of war. So everywhere there is the reminder that even such a story as this takes place in the world of all of us,

in questa assai piú oscura che serena
vita mortal, tutta d'invidia piena.

(IV. i)

[In this our life, more dark than bright,
all full of envy.]

And at any moment something might happen,

mandando or questo or quel giú ne l'inferno
a dar notizia del viver moderno.

(XVI. lxxxiii)

[Dispatching now this one now that one to Hell,
to let it be known what modern life is like.]

Such a consciousness is enough to demand the full capacities of realism in the support of this apparently fantastic matter, and wonderfully enough the astonishing use of the divine figures of Christianity strengthens the poem's contemporaneity. It is not merely that their use avoids the associations of antiquity and of antiquity alone that belong to Zeus and the others of his company, but that the immediacy and the grounds of the intervention of Christian divinities in stories of the Crusaders signify an intervention in the life of the Este court itself, in Ariosto's own Ferrara, and God himself says, at the end of the story of Isabella,

Per l'avvenir vo' che ciascun ch'aggia
il nome tuo, sia de sublime ingegno,
e sia bella, gentil, cortese e saggia,
e di vera onestade arrivi al segno:
onde materia agli scrittori caggia
di celebrare il nome inclito e degno;
tal che Parnasso, Pindo et Elicone
sempre Issabella, Issabella risuone.

(XXIX. xxix)

That for her sake that dide of this name last,
Who ever shall hereafter beare that name,
Shall be both wise and continent and chast,
Of faultlesse manners, and of spotlesse fame,

Let writers strive to make their glorie last,
And oft in prose and verse record the same,
Let *Hellicon*, *Pindus*, *Parnassus* hill,
Sound *Isabella*, *Isabella* still. (XXIX. 31)

The clear distinction between the habitation of God and the world of men, the barrier between us and the moon and what takes place there and the vast space above that where God and the angels live, separated as clearly as in Lucian from our planet, all this has the effect of making the mingling of the worlds more real when it does happen, for by such a relationship all must be most circumstantially described. As it is in that superb journey to the moon in the thirty-fourth canto, or as in the words of God that have just been quoted. Thus, since Divinity so patently enters history, if there is ever allegory it need not depend upon a Platonic scale in which abstractions gradually ascend towards ideal reality. The concreteness of matters that in other ways of thought would be believed to be intangible makes that superfluous. So there is the simple fact always for the evidence of God's reality. John the Baptist, for example, reminds Astolfo of what he owes to God, and the words he uses are entirely acceptable to the general sense of the poet himself:

che né il tuo corno, né il cavallo alato
ti valea, se de Dio non t'era dato. (XXXIV. lvi)

For neither could thy horn nor winged steed
Without Gods help stand thee in any steed.

Astolfo knew this very well—

Né l'angel di Dio,
né son Messia novel, né dal ciel vegno:
ma son mortale e peccatore anch'io,
di tanta grazia a me concessa indegno.
Io farò ogn'opra acciò che 'l mostro rio,
per morte o fuga, io ti levi del regno.
S'io il fo, me non, ma Dio ne loda solo,
che per tuo aiuto qui mi drizzò il volo.
(XXXIII. cxvii)

Nor Angell I, nor new *Messias* am,
Nor come from heav'n, but mortall man am I,
And thrall to sinne, unworthy so high name;
But for your sake my best skill I will trie,
To kill or drive those fools from whence they came,
Which if I do, give God, not me the praise,
That for your help did hither guide my waies.
(XXXIII. 108)

These are almost the words Spenser uses in one of the passages closest to his central thought,[1] but how different the sense!

His be the praise, that this atchieu'ment wrought,
Who made my hand the organ of his might;
More then goodwill to me attribute nought:
For all I did, I did but as I ought.
(II. i. 33)

In Ariosto they mean only that any man is the child of God and in the great frame of things he would be foolish to claim much credit for himself, so small a part of it all. In Spenser's conception there is the idea of the immanence of God, and no miracle, no vast interruption in the laws of the world attends His revelations or Arthur's coming when he represents grace to some endangered knight. All is, hopefully, a seamless world, and not, as here—

Poi le fece veder, come non fusse
alcun, se non in Dio, vero contento,
e ch'eran l'altre transitorie e flusse
speranze umane, e di poco momento.
(XXIV. lxxxix)

And prov'd and shew'd by reasons evident,
That worldly things are vaine and have no hold,
Alone in God is joy and true content.
(XXIV. 72)

In Ariosto God will, as it were, unashamedly mingle with the particulars of the world, and He speaks Italian. So it is that the

[1] See above, pp. 72–73.

resources of realism are drawn on and the values of the human world get their full emphasis, and those particularly of marriage. Too often, of course, the hopes of men and women must be fulfilled in Heaven, as for Isabella—

> Dio cosí disse, e fe' serena intorno
> l'aria, e tranquillo il mar piú che mai fusse.
> Fe' l'alma casta al terzo ciel ritorno,
> e in braccio al suo Zerbin si ricondusse.
>
> (XXIX. xxx)
>
> Thus said the Hy'st, and then there did ensew
> A wondrous calme in waters and in aire,
> The chast soule up into the third heav'n flew,
> Where Zerbin was, to that she did repaire.
>
> (XXIX. 32)

But even such a faith makes clear the tragic possibilities in a world of heroes and lovers. The madness of Orlando, which is but the sum of the madness of all lovers, is madness, of course, a false vision of things, and yet it is also universal. Once Orlando hears the sound of angels—

> E voci e suoni d'angeli concordi
> tosto in aria s'udîr che l'alma uscío.
>
> (XLII. xiv)
>
> Straight Angels voices with most sweet accord,
> Were heard the while his spirit did ascend.

As has been well said, "Orlando alone hears the heavenly melody, he alone sees Paradise before him, but he does not rejoice, he weeps, this hero whom we have seen from the very beginning dreaming and weeping, and the poet never tires of insisting on his complaint."[1] But the plaint is also Ariosto's. It is he who has tested the falseness of the vision and has moved us so deeply in telling us about it. Momigliano summed the matter up: "The effect is tragic, but of that perplexed and indefinable kind that belongs to extraordinary spectacles and of poetry that seems to be only a dream."[2]

[1] Translated from Fumagalli, *Unità Fantastica dell'Orlando Furioso*, p. 63.
[2] Translated from *Saggio su l' "Orlando Furioso,"* p. 47.

It comes to this, that the *Orlando Furioso* is a poem in which it is possible to praise a man by calling him "umano" (XLIV. vi) and, by the fact of loving, to call him "onesto" (V. lxiv) and wretched. The men and women in their quests for love and honour are not like the figures of Spenser's poem, or many another romance, wanderers in a forest following some holy light, but in the forests of Ariosto ("bosche selve" he calls them again and again) they are individuals in a slaughter-house about to be abandoned, half the time mad with jealousy or love, and the great figure that gives his name to the poem, raging, knowing no paths out of his madness, no road away from himself, not knowing the one thing that might be some help, that there is no way out.[1]

[1] Dè Sanctis and later Croce have done so much to insist that there is no mind here worth the name, and indeed no content to the poem, views shared, it appears by J. W. Mackail and Mr. C. S. Lewis, that one ought, I think, to regard more steadily words like these of Carducci's: "Ma come si può parlare d'ironia intenzionale dell' Ariosto? dell' Ariosto, che al personaggio di Carlomagno, mortificato dalla famigliarità birichina dei piazzaiuolo di Firenze, restituì la maestà d'imperatore e il contegno d'eroe? dell' Ariosto che l'Astolfo fatto buffone dal Boiardo rifece cavalliere d'avventure e miracoli, pronto a tutto affrontare, le porte così dell'inferno come del paradiso, con quella sua seria audacia inglese che lo costituisce degno istrumento della providenza alla salute d'Orlando? dell' Ariosto che in Orlando il peccato dell' amore, peccato per l'eroe e pe' l cristiano, punisce con la terribil pazzia? E come si può parlare d'ironia continua e finale dinanzi alla terribilità tragica di quella pazzia in quella più che descrizione e narrazione epica, la quale dalla minuta e fedele osservazione dei succedentisi momenti psicologici va a passo a passo crescendo vorticosa e vertiginosa e finisce in uno scoppio titanico? dinanzi all'eroica grandezza dell'ultimo abbatimento fra i tre re saracini e i tre paladini, e alla mossa, tutta di cuore, del poeta, su 'l cadere di Brandimarte,

> Padre del ciel, dà fra gli eletti tuoi
> Al martir tuo fedele omai ricetto?"

("L'Orlando Furioso," in *La Vita Italiana nel Cinquecento: II. Letteratura*, Milan, 1894, p. 348.)

The phrases of a more recent critic also carry weight in this matter of the tragic emphasis of the poem: "E bisogna, d'altra parte, oltre i colpi meravigliosi, non perdere di vista la pazzia pietosa di Orlando: Orlando inselvatichito, Orlando che si trascina dietro la cavalla sfiancata e morta, Orlando dissennato al punto che è peggio che stolida bestia. Questo aspetto pietoso di Orlando pazzo è il più serio commento alla serietà della sua passione amorosa e perciò alla serietà

Orlando's defeat only magnifies the dilemma of the romantic desire, of the love of what may be unattainable.[1] One can see that in such a matter there would be great interest for Spenser, and how the range of Ariosto's poem, the hundreds of characters, the

della sua follia." (Raffaele Spongano, *La Prosa di Galileo e Altri Scritti*, Firenze: G. D'Anna, 1949, pp. 57–58.)

Another recent writer comments with considerable power on the tragic feeling in the poem in such a way as to help show how Orlando's madness is central to the structure of the poem: "Il suo [Ariosto's] dramma è, preso alla lettera, dramma di redenzione cristiana, come la Divina Commedia, ma le affermazioni dell'Ariosto suonano a vuoto; a esse è ribelle la creazione artistica si può dire in toto. Infatti la storia dell' impazzimento ha procedimento psicologico a base naturalistica, e quella del rinsavimento si affida al miracoloso-magico, non solo senza brivido di soprannaturale, ma con larga vena comica e fin grottesca. Soltanto nella terza evoluzione d'Orlando, l'Ariosto ha veramente ravvicinato il mondo della fede al suo Eroe, ma non per grazia divina, si ancora per un processo psicologico naturale: Orlando risorto dal sepolcro della ragione dove può rifugiare, morta Brandimarte, la sua anima mortalmente stanca? nelle vecchie credenze, nell'antica fede. Ritorna al suo Cristo perchè il mondo l'ha tradito, vi ritorna con la passione chiusa e sognatrice ch'è propria della sua idealista natura, perciò ode i canti degli angeli, vede schiudersi il Cielo, mentre tiene fra le sue braccia l'amico morente e piange. Si prepara il martire di Roncisvalle, ma per un'evoluzione di spirito naturale, da un'arte in tutto umana, che può accogliere voci di mistica ascesi con risonanze accorate e solenni, solo come espressioni di una deserta angoscia, l'estrema. Illusioni di un mondo soprasensible necessarie quando qui son cadute tutte le illusioni. Illusione, condizione sine qua non della vita e tormento della vita, apparenza e sostanza, miraggio e realtà . . . siamo nel foco ideologico e fantastico che animò e irragiò tutto il Poema." (Fumagalli, *Unità Fantastica dell' Orlando Furioso*, pp. 66–67.)

[1] It was often the condition of Orlando to be alone with his thoughts, as Fumagalli has remarked ("solo col suo fantasma," p. 31), a reminder once more of the circumstances of isolation that seem so often to be proper to certain kinds of heroes in romances. A similar observation has been made of Chrétien's Launcelot in the *Conte de la Charrete:* "Chrétien ha rappresentato poeticamente un uomo che, nella sua natura meditativa, cerca la donna lontana, la raggiunge con le grandi forze della sua anima, e la richiama a sé dal Regno da cui non si torna; la crea come sacra, e per raggiungerla si distacca da ogni amore di sé, da ogni pregiudizio sociale, facendose intorno una grande solitudine." (Lorenza Maranini, " 'Queste' e amore cortese nel 'Chevalier de la Charrete,' " *Rivista di Letterature Moderne*, I [1951], 222.)

Following Gilson and his own reading of Augustine in taking the idea of the romantic quest to be the love of God in oneself, Mario Casella writes with

complexity of the plot, the superb narrative style, magnifying that tragic conception, must have challenged him. Above all, that Orlando should have been defeated, one who was the example of "a good gouernour and a vertuous man"—his hero must conquer.

TASSO AND THE PASTORAL

De Sanctis' comment on the enchanted forest of the *Gerusalemme Liberata*, that this is Tasso himself,[1] is wonderfully just. Yet the forest is but another vision of the pastoral world of the *Aminta*. It is as if Tasso in the *Liberata* had somehow to combine the world of innocence and the world of fear and passion and madness, to the balance in which it could be seen that love in its genesis in humans and in its journey towards chaos and death ever deserved the name of innocence, and the endowment of immortality. He was of course pursuing this conception without the support of philosophy, as Spenser also was in the Pastorella story, and Shakespeare everywhere. Spenser at many places tried his hand at Neo-Platonic arguing to give a way of accounting for the divinity of what might also on occasion be thought of as hellish. In the *Epithalamion* and some of the sonnets he provided a base in the simplicity of common experience and even in the acknowledgment of a Christian way of looking at marriage. But it was the non-philosophical bent he needed to follow for what was truest to his mind and poetry, and to show the power of innocence to survive in the world.

considerable persuasiveness to the effect that Cervantes found in the *Orlando Furioso* this same perception to help him to his own idealizations: "Il Cervantes ha visto nell' *Orlando Furioso* ciò che non hanno visto i critici numerosi che si sono posti idealmente di fronte a quel capolavoro. Ivi l'irrazionale poetico, che è puro amore e principio metafisico della personalità umana, è osservato come il problèma di vita che ciascuno deve rissolvere e risolve con l'intelletto che gli è proprio. L'Ariosto pone a centro del suo poema quell' irrazionale che va giustificato in se stesso, e di cui la ragione umana non sa rendersi ragione se non rivivendolo in sè con amore. . . . L'Ariosto ha collocato nel regno della pura fantasia quell' irrazionale poetico che il Cervantes inserisce nella storia contemporanea spagnola. La differenza non è piccola. . . . (*Il Chisciotte*, Firenze: Le Monnier, 1938, I, 225.)

[1] See below, pp. 181–82.

Tasso and Spenser both moved back and forth between the romantic and the pastoral scenes. One might say that the enchanted forest of Tasso and the Arcadian scene are always changing into each other, and that in Spenser Faerie Land is now the Terre Gaste, now Broceliande, at another time Arcadia. The happiest balance in *The Faerie Queene* was achieved in the Pastorella story, and here, it seems, Spenser brought over from a Greek romance some of its lucidity.[1] Whatever the resources, Spenser's achievement here within a romance brought the pastoral to a depth of spiritual insight not expressed before this, I think, in literature.

Calidore forgot his duty once he came to a quiet place in the midst of the forest and he stayed there. The charm, in Meliboe's perfect words was,

> This lowly quiet life, which I inherite here.
>
> (VI. ix. 25)

It was this at first that kept him, and the absence of ambition and corruption and perhaps toil, and afterwards it was love. And he reversed the usual disciplines leading to gallantry, the attainment of the virtues of knightliness that would gain a mistress, for here he needed to learn not to be a knight, but to be a shepherd, not to engage in war, and by nature's courtesy alone to prove his nobility and love. So he put his arms aside although he still needed to know how to wrestle and to kill a tiger with his crook. Hunting remained his trade, and he would always remember how to stand and fight alone against a host of villains. It was not ever his courage and skill that was to be at issue, but the struggle for power in the great world and the life of ambition.

What marked his love for Pastorella was its simplicity, an attachment as in nature and as if without words, and not to be moved by disaster. She herself, the admired of all the Graces, in her perfection knew no change, and Calidore in knowing her conceived of none.

[1] Edwin Greenlaw has an illuminating discussion of the relation of the Pastorella episode to *Daphnis and Chloe* and Sidney's *Arcadia* in "Shakespeare's Pastorals," *Studies in Philology*, XIII (1916), 123–29.

When Calidore came by chance upon the Graces—

> It was an hill plaste in an open plaine,
> That round about was bordered with a wood—
> (VI. x. 6)

he felt as one to whom they might have shown themselves in visions. It is Colin's words that say something like this when Calidore asked him,

> Tell me, what mote these dainty Damzels be,
> Which here with thee doe make their pleasant playes?
> Right happy thou, that mayst them freely see:
> But why when I them saw, fled they away from me?
>
> Not I so happy, answerd then that swaine,
> As thou vnhappy, which them thence didst chace,
> Whom by no means thou canst recall againe,
> For being gone, none can them bring in place,
> But whom they of them selues list so to grace.
> (VI. x. 19–20)

For a moment he had been in some blessed and unforseeable state, the state of love in which the servants of Venus appeared to him and graced him—

> Those three to men all gifts of grace do graunt,
> And all, that *Venus* in her selfe doth vaunt,
> Is borrowed of them—
> (VI. x. 15)

summoned perhaps by poetry and adoration, Colin's and his. They were not gods but as real, beautiful and simple in their nakedness, quiet, almost abstracted in silence as it is in Botticelli's Love and Spring where none is thinking of speaking. Here there is simply dancing to Colin's melody:

> But that faire one,
> That in the midst was placed parauaunt,
> Was she to whom that shepheard pypt alone,
> That made him pipe so merrily, as neuer none.

She was to weete that iolly Shepheards lasse,
Which piped there vnto that merry rout,
That iolly shepheard, which there piped, was
Poore *Colin Clout* (who knowes not *Colin Clout?*)
He pypt apace, whilest they him daunst about.
Pype iolly shepheard, pype thou now apace
Vnto thy loue, that made thee low to lout:
Thy loue is present there with thee in place,
Thy loue is there aduanst to be another Grace.

(VI. x. 15–16)

From that sight Calidore returned to find the wreckage of his hosts' home. Then he came upon the piles of dead, and the wounded Pastorella. At first he was ready to tear his own flesh at the sight of the destruction and with the sense of his loss. Then he regained himself, and finally went on to rescue Pastorella and to have vengeance. So we see that there had been no enervation after all in this life he had been living with the shepherds, for after such deeds he then took up his other duties. When these are done we expect him to return to marry Pastorella, now known for her proper birth.

That is all. There is no mention when the book ends of such a marriage or of the permanence of their relationship, yet in the books to follow their story must have required a description like none of the other loves of *The Faerie Queene*. For while Britomart and Arthur and the others despaired, their loves as we know them were mostly in the seeking and little in the fulfilment. This one is as it were fulfilled in the beginning, untroubled and simple, as of the pure in heart. Yet none of the other figures knew grief so real or wounds so truly bloody as these endured, or slaughter or the loss of parents or the destruction of homes. None of the others belong quite so much to the sufferings of the real world. For Calidore and Pastorella the vicissitudes are as fierce and meaningless as in life, and yet their love and cherishing is so perfect, so inaccessible to distraction, and so un-self-questioning, it obviously depends on a quite other loyalty than that which questions itself.

They apparently knew nothing even through pain of what Tasso and Shakespeare and Racine were so fatally instructed in:

> C'est moi, prince, c'est moi dont l'utile secours
> Vous eût du Labyrinthe enseigné les detours.
>
> (*Phèdre*, II. v. 655–6)

The story, the names, the movement of the verse say it all, and there is no comment and nothing even from Plato to help us accept what we are persuaded to take at its own terms, the perfection of nature. Like those wonder-working heroines of Shakespeare, Pastorella and all her world are put quite simply before us for our acceptance. And what this means, in the midst of this great crowd of wandering knights and ladies in this most various scene, what this special pastoral innocence means to it all is that this is something new, something the pastoral had never expressed before.

Spenser, beginning as he had, following after Theocritus and Mantuan, was caught up in the seriousness of the pastoral after Montemayor and Tasso, as everybody was for almost a century, yet struck out differently. Even as in a poem modelled on Ariosto's he set out to make his own Protestant and patriotic work, so in the celebration of love, in the Pastorella story and in the *Hymnes* he brought to his conception of holiness and justice and all the virtues a conception of love that belonged with all of them. It was a different perfection than Tasso's and a complete answer to Ariosto's fury, and he meant it to be equal to all the attacks of mutability.

The great poem, centring on the wandering of its heroes, and on magnificence and glory and national greatness, will also express happiness. The poem must take that great scene of the hundreds of knights and ladies and magicians and slowly make a world where all that is said in Ariosto that is true will be said again, and especially all that is said about the richness and variety and deceitfulness of life, although Spenser will leave out something of the intellectuality and much of the Catholic temperament. He will transform all this gradually, although the absence of wit will be immediately made known, for he does his work mostly by a singleness of mind, plainness, a certain still undefeated aspiration towards the heroic, and something zealous, too, one may here call Puritan. And although there will be everywhere in the poem the sad sense of time and decay, the effort of his work will be to show that love makes the vast variety of things a comprehensive vision. The whole conception depends on this:

For loue is Lord of truth and loialtie,
(*Hymne of Love*, 176)

Whatever the interest he has in Plato, for all the chance he gives his mind to play over the vistas and meanings of that kind of thought, he remains a simpler sort of humanist. However one may transfer the Nurse's words to Britomart, that love is guided by Providence,[1] to all the others in the poem there is no recognition that love is a divine rage, or that passion has anything of the nature of Venus in Spenser's description of the Garden of Adonis. It does not possess the authority of the guiding principle of the universe. In Calidore and Pastorella there is nothing of Plato or Lucretius or Ovid, and the bandits are not satyrs or wood-gods. Instead of divinity, one finds the innocence of humanity, surviving where even Orlando would have been destroyed.

For Tasso love must be victorious over any circumstance, and in thus differing from Ariosto he is like Spenser, but the nature of the victory Tasso conceived rested on a depth and complexity of feeling different from anything Spenser was to entertain, yet it was to lead the pastoral conception into its most moving expression in European poetry.

A modern critic has observed that *Rinaldo*, Tasso's first ambitious poem, is devoted to "the new ideal of marriage, founded on the laws of love,"[2] and that it is the inspiration of this idea that qualifies Tasso's relation of the story in which a young knight is trying to prove himself worthy of a lady. The observation is true, I think, and it is worth while looking at *Rinaldo* with this in mind for the light it throws on the later works and the ideas of love expressed there. And there are still other considerations that lead us toward a consideration of this poem, and apart from Spenser's

[1] See below, p. 187.

[2] Errico Proto, *Sul Rinaldo di Torquato Tasso*, Naples, 1895, p. 279.

particular knowledge of it.[1] Tasso begins with a romance, later there is the miraculous pastoral work, and finally there is the poem that is deeply different from that first romantic work and yet with still so much of the romantic necessity informing it. By the end he departed from the romantic form to such a degree that one must say that it is the *Rinaldo* which more resembles *The Faerie Queene* than the *Liberata*. But in the poem on the crusades the quest for love and for perfection will be still so close to the conception of his first work that it is also right to affirm that the heroic figures of the *Liberata* are in one respect at least like the knights of Spenser, all are conditions of a single figure and all merge in the idea of the greatest of knights,[2] "a gentleman or noble person," and in both works it is exactly true to say that glory is "the general intention." In Tasso, too, there must be a settlement of the terms on which the romantic and the pastoral scene shall become part of a single conception, in a poem in which the quest for glory and the acknowledgment of innocence shall be understood to live in harmony, if only for a moment, in this world. And if Spenser begins with Ariosto, to improve upon that poem, to carry the idea of virtue and the idea of love along together to some victorious end, he will go on from the *Rinaldo* and the *Aminta*, to an achievement that will in the end contradict Tasso and his idea of the holiness of love. And as one estimates the magnitude of Tasso's achievement one is able to perceive the vigour of Spenser's invention and the originality of his divergence.

What is perhaps most interesting about the *Rinaldo* is the simplicity and clarity of the idea—a younger brother, overshadowed in fame, goes forth to achieve glory and thus to be worthy of love. He starts out blindly, in time he finds a lady, he proves himself, and after many adventures and even the adventure of unfaithfulness he returns and is married.

[1] The Variorum edition of Spenser records some parallels.

[2] "... i molti cavalieri sono considerati nel mio poema come membra d'un corpo, del quale è capo Goffredo, Rinaldo destra; sí che in un certo modo si può dire anco unitá d'agente, non che d'azione." (From a letter to Scipione Gonzaga, in *Torquato Tasso: Prose*, ed. Francesco Flora, Milan, 1935, p. 576.)

As the poem gets under way the marvellousness of the adventures he encounters begins to steal our interest, but for all the skill in which we are told of the fantastic, our interest in the simplicity of Rinaldo's purpose is kept alive by its essential lack of complication, of all that deviousness in the heart and mind of figures of more mature imaginations. If, like Tennyson's hero, Rinaldo had been setting out with the Grail as his announced goal, one would be prepared for all the power of simplicity, but here it is unexpected, the young warrior starting out so blindly, and so one knows that there is something especially good and beautiful here.

The succession of marvellous events at the beginning and throughout is as if Tasso were a connoisseur in these matters, and had picked out some of the most astonishing he had read about. To begin with, he has incorporated the explicitly Arthurian material more intimately in the poem than either Boiardo or Ariosto did, and in picking out the most astonishing incidents he has emphasized more what in them is mysterious rather than what might lead to allegory, and he increases the mystery by something of that passionate attention to detail that was later to be still more powerful. The vividness of the statue of Tristan nodding his head,

> china 'l capo la statua di Tristano;[1] (III. 64)
>
> The statue of Tristan bowed his head.[2]

a sudden fissure in the earth, and a chariot rising out of it, drawn by four black horses breathing flame (IV. 57 ff.); a woman speaking in a dream (IX. 82–84); an enchanted boat:

> Sen vanno al lido i due guerrieri insieme
> e rendon quivi il fatal legno carco.
> Quel, come sente il pondo il qual lo preme,
> si muove quasi stral ch'esca da l'arco:
> frangesi l'onda e mormorando freme
> tutta spumante sotto 'l curvo incarco;
> intauto fugge e si dilegua il lito,
> sí che da gli occhi omai tutto è sparito. (VIII. 24)

[1] *Rinaldo*, ed. Luigi Bonfigli, Bari, 1936.

[2] The translations from the *Rinaldo* are mine.

> The two warriors went together to the shore and there untied the fatal wooden bark. When it felt their weight pressing it, it moved forth like an arrow from the bow. The wave broke beneath its bow and all foaming gave forth a murmuring sound. Meanwhile, the shore was left behind and got smaller and smaller until finally it was lost to sight.

And then:

> Non pria dal legno ognun fu dismontato
> che quel ratto lasciò la terra a tergo,
> e da l'incanto per lo mar guidato
> tornò veloce ne l'antico albergo.
>
> (VIII. 47)

> Not until everyone was disembarked did the swift boat leave the land at its back, and guided through the sea by incantation it returned swiftly to its old harbour.

The fantastic matters gain a special beauty from the way Tasso tells the story, for almost everything takes place by chance. At the beginning Rinaldo starts out aimlessly, *errando per lo bosco* (I. 32). He meets another knight, and together

> prendono il calle,
> ove tòrse il destrier la lor ventura.
>
> (II. 47)

> They took the way where chance turned their charger.

The knight's quest is self-assumed, it is no burden laid on him by God or King, and although his enemies are of all kinds and include magicians and Saracens, there is no devil, no principle of evil in the outer world to oppose him. As in the later poem the Saracen maiden has it within her power to accept Christianity, and Rinaldo will depend upon himself, and chance, for victory. The absence of dominating supernatural forces gives the fantastic adventures the quality of naïveness—by chance two knights meet under a tree, by chance they come across an old man who has something important to say to them, and later they come to a stream just as the triumphal water-chariot they need happens along. There is nothing crude here, as if the writer did not know his business, nor is chance given its part, as sometimes in Spenser, to help the allegory. There is rather the possibility that chance represents a principle in the universe, and but for that suggestion the charm of the events would be wholly naïve.

The main idea, of course, is that Rinaldo should prove worthy of the lady he serves, and his story in its fundamental conception is what Ker, writing of *Sir Gawaine and the Green Knight*, called "a chivalrous *Pilgrim's Progress*."[1]

The hero trusts himself—

> Nel còr consiston l'armi,
> onde il forte non è chi mai disarmi—
> (II. 28)
>
> In the heart are the arms a brave man never
> puts aside—

but not enough. He must strengthen his faith. In the desire of glory and on fire with love, he must overcome wild beasts blocking his way, endure the trials of chastity, visit a kind of Earthly Paradise and a vale of grief, and somehow we are to understand that at the end he has proved himself and is finally worthy of an adventure and a reward that was not within his reach at the beginning. And our sense of his progress is effected without allegory, although the advances Rinaldo makes are clearly comparable to the regeneration of several of the knights of *The Faerie Queene*.

It is somehow affecting to remind ourselves that the *Innamora-*

[1] *English Literature: Medieval* (Home University Library), p. 164. From a slightly different point of view: ". . . è bello vedere come al Tasso giovinetto risuscisse di trarre da un *cantare* del ciclo di *Carlo* un *romanzo* del ciclo di Artù, nel quale Rinaldo, pur ritenendo la sua impronta originaria, pur chiamato Paladino, è trasformato però in un cavaliere errante, fedele alla sua dama ed all'onore." (Proto, *Sul Rinaldo di Torquato Tasso*, p. 279.)

mento del Rinaldo, and the same story in *The Four Sons of Aymon*, from which Tasso's story is derived, have much less of that sense of the maturing of the knight. There, too, is a kind of anarchy to begin with, and a falling away from the Emperor. Reynaud, anxious either for vengeance or forgiveness, wanders through the world from one adventure to another, but he has nothing that could be called a mission. What interests us in his story is simply whether he will be able to keep his balance, losing himself neither in bitterness nor apathy. We want to discover if, without the support of an emperor to whom he can be loyal, indeed deprived of any object of loyalty, he may yet remain a brave and courteous knight. That substantial anarchy is also the beginning of *Rinaldo*, although here the story of the younger, unfavoured brother suggests a kind of primeval injustice as much as anything else. But Tasso was able to conceive of a less degenerate world than that of *The Four Sons of Aymon*, and chiefly through the values he set on marriage.[1] The language describing the wedding at the end of the story expresses this informing virtue:

> Spinti i fidi amador da questi detti,
> e dal desir ch'in lor n'è giá di paro,
> tenner concordi a' maritali effetti,
> ch'in presenza d'ognun si celebrâro:
> fûro i lor còr da gentil laccio astretti,
> ch'Amore e Castitá doce annodâro:
> sorrise Giove, e con secondo tuono
> veder gran luce, udir fe' lieto suono.
>
> (XII. 87)

[1] "C'è ancora a osservare, a lode del poeta, che in questo romanzo (come osserva il Canello) informa anch'egli l'ideale nuovo del matrimonio, fondato sulle leggi d'amore. Altrove osservammo quali fossero questi romanzi iniziatori del nuovo indirizzo ideale: or qui diremo che il *Tassino* segue l'ideale voluto incarnar dall'Ariosto nel romanzo di Ruggiero e Bradamante, e l'ideale, che scaturisce dall'*Amadigi*: cioè di un cavaliere, che col proprio valore si rende degno della dama, e ad essa si congiunge, non per calcolo, nè per ragion di Stato, ma per mutuo amore, sul quale dovea fondarsi il nuovo matrimonio, poi che l'antico era stato distrutto dall'adulterio manifesto o tollerato." (Proto, *Sul Rinaldo di Torquato Tasso*, p. 279.)

> Moved by these words and the desire that was already in both of them equally, the faithful lovers agreed to the marriage arrangements and that they were to be celebrated in the presence of all. Their hearts were bound by the gentle cord that Love and sweet Chastity had tied. Jove smiled, and with the thunder following they saw a great light and they heard a joyful sound.

> giá spargeva Imeneo co' i vaghi amori
> fiori e frondi nel suol, canti nel cielo,
> quando di propria man Venere bella
> congiunse in un Rinaldo e la donzella.
> (XII. 88)

> Now Hymen with the delightful Loves scattered flowers and leaves on the ground and hurled their songs into the sky when lovely Venus with her own hand made Rinaldo and the maiden one.

> godete il ben che casto Amor v'inspira,
> e l'oneste dolcezze e i gaudi santi.
> (XII. 89)

> Enjoy the good that chaste Love inspires and the honest sweets and the holy joys.

Whatever support the word chastity can give the quality of the love in this poem, all has something of the richness of the scene in which the marriage takes place. It is richer than the setting of the Pastorella episode, although in so many other ways the comparison is necessary, Tasso and Spenser alike differing from Ariosto in uniting the dream of an Earthly Paradise with the ideal of marriage. Here, as in pastoral poetry,

> Quivi non querci e pini, abeti o faggi,
> ma lauri, mirti e vaghi altri arbuscelli
> difendono il terren da' caldi raggi
> con gli odorati lor verdi capelli;

quivi nei còr piú duri e piú selvaggi
destan dolce pensier vezzosi augelli,
che, scherzando su' rami e su le fronde,
soavemente a l'un l'altro risponde.
(VII. 56)

Here neither oaks nor pines nor firs nor
beeches, but laurels, myrtles, and other
delightful shrubs protect the soil from
the hot beams with their fragrant green
locks. Here in the hardest and wildest
hearts the graceful birds wake sweet thoughts
as darting from branch to branch and through
the leaves they sweetly answer one another.

The beauty of nature, a festival with choirs of beautiful women dancing, among them a princess disguised as a shepherdess, all this is made so simply harmonious that it seems nature is overcome by love, and that love rules even the humbly placed. This idea goes farther here than in Boiardo or Spenser either one, and it is closer to Lucretius than to most of the followers of the *stil nuovo.* But here, as in the rest of Tasso's poetry, there can be no contradiction. The shepherd may turn out to be royal, but that is merely for the pleasure of surprise. Love itself is royal, not least in its animality, and when the shepherd comes to the Queen—

ne le sue labbra le mie labbra impressi—
(V. 52)

I pressed my lips against hers—

we understand that the sensuality of love is part of the sensuality of nature.

To go on from the *Rinaldo* to the *Aminta* and then the *Gerusalemme Liberata,* concerned with the questions of religion and glory and love, is to see how Tasso as the years pass takes more and more of the world into his understanding. At the same time a question is again raised about romances, and how they might, as in the *Rinaldo*, make place for so much the pastoral can express. Such a study helps us as with Spenser to understand something of the fundamental passion and urgency in these great, epic efforts of the Renaissance. Tasso, too, has magnificent intentions, the romance in its simpler forms will not quite serve them, and the pastoral, in his most perfect achievement, speaks only part of his meaning. So he goes on finally to the great poem on the Crusades, to exploit all that he has until then developed. The issues of Catholicism and the Counter-Reformation are as pressingly important to him as are Protestant ideas to Spenser, and if political matters are of less consequence it is because his poetry is always closer to desperation. But for both, the central thing, the religiousness, depends at the beginning and at the end, and step by step, on the importance of love, on its significance, on the bonds between men and women and the passions that bind them, and on the elation of these passions to divinity. The pastoral gives these explorations extraordinary authority.

The story of the *Aminta* is of a lover and a maiden who is interested neither in him nor in love itself. In trying to win her Aminta attracts instead of love her fury and is half persuaded he cannot go on living. And so depressed, when word comes that wolves have killed her, he throws himself from a cliff.

Passionate as his love was, he was nevertheless solicitous, and this tenderness alone distinguishes him from the Satyr who is also in love with Silvia. The wood creature preferred her consent to his attentions, but when she continued to repulse him he lost patience and ran off with her, tied her naked to a tree, and was about to force her when Aminta fortunately came up and drove him away. But even so great a service did not move Silvia to care for the one who had rescued her and, on the contrary, the shame of her experience made her act still more arrogantly towards him. Aminta, powerless in the face of this cruelty, could make no gesture of resentment or violence except against himself.

Yet his love for her is as sensual as the Satyr's, for whom instinct is the only law, and for whom violence is good because his strength, which comes from Nature, is by that fact itself good.[1] Aminta's love is as sensual but more self-regarding, and its tenderness is perhaps voluptuousness. The differences thus are slight, and this is one of the causes of the power of the poem, that all are agreed on the nature of love and all speak for the poet:

Mira là quel colombo
Che con dolce susurro lusingando
Bacia la sua compagna;
Odi quel lusignuolo
Che va di ramo in ramo
Cantando: *Io amo, io amo;* e, se no 'l sai,
La biscia or lascia il suo veleno e corre
Cupida a 'l suo amatore;
Van le tigri in amore,

1 Usa ciascuno
Quell'arme che gli ha date la natura
Per sua salute: il cervo adopra il corso,
Il leone gli artigli, ed il bavoso
Cinghiale il dente; e son potenza ed arme
Ne la donna bellezza e leggiadria.
Io, perché non per mia salute adopro
La vïolenza, se mi fe' natura
Atto a far vïolenze ed a rapire?

(*Aminta*, ed. Luigi Fassò, Florence: Sansoni, 1946, II. i. 72–80.)

let each creature use
Those armes that Nature for his ayde hath giu'n him,
The Hart his speede, the Lyon his strong pawe,
The foaming Bore his tuske; the womans armes
And powre lye in her beauty, and gracefull shape;
I, since my strength is the best helpe I haue,
And am by nature fit for deedes of force,
Will for reward of all my loue misspent,
Force this proud cruell to my owne content.

(*Torquato Tasso's Aminta Englisht*, by Henry Reynolds, London, 1628, Sig. C_2.)

Eugenio Donadoni in his interpretation and criticism of this matter is, I believe, both precise and just: "Unica legge è la Natura: e l'istinto: e pel Satiro è buona la violenza, poichè Natura gli ha data la forza (II, 79 sgg.). L'uomo adoprerà la ragione; ma sempre allo stesso scopo: di possedere, di godere." (*Torquato Tasso, Saggio Critico*, 3rd ed., Florence: La Nuova Italia, 1946, p. 123.)

Ama il leon superbo; e tu sol, fera
Più che tutte le fere,
Albergo gli denieghi ne 'l tuo petto.
Ma che dico leoni e tigri e serpi,
Che pur han sentimento? amano ancora
Gli arbori. Veder puoi con quanto affetto
E con quanti iterati abbracciamenti
La vite s'avviticchia a 'l suo marito;
L'abete ama l'abete, il pino il pino,
L'orno per l'orno e per la salce il salce
E l'un per l'altro faggio arde e sospira.
Quella quercia, che pare
Sì ruvida e selvaggia,
Sente anch'ella il potere
De l'amoroso foco; e se tu avessi
Spirto e senso d'amore, intenderesti
I suoi muti sospiri. Or tu da meno
Esser vuoi de le piante,
Per non essere amante?

(I. i. 137–64)

behold that Turtle there
With what a wooing murmur he sighes loue
To his belou'de; harke of yon Nitingall
That hops from bough to bough,
Singing I loue I loue; nay more then these,
The speckled Serpent layes his venim by,
And greedy runnes to' imbrace his loued one;
The Tygar loues, and the proud Lion too;
Thou onely sauadge more then sauadge beasts
Barr'st against loue thy more-then-yron brest.
But what speake I of Lions, Tygars, Snakes,
That sensible ar? why all these trees doe loue;
See with what amorous and redoubled twinings
The louing Vine her husband faire intangles;
The Beech tree loues the Beech, the Pine the Pine,
The Elme the Elme loues, and the Willows too
A mutuall languish for each other feele.

That Oake that seemes so rough and so impenitrable,
Doth no lesse feele the force of amorous flame;
And hadst thou but the spirit and sence of loue,
His hidden language thou wouldst vnderstand.
Wilt thou be lesse and worse then trees and plants,
In being thus an enimy to Loue?

(Sig. B)

This rapture, almost mesmeric in Tasso's accent, gives Aminta's boast to have been like Orpheus more persuasion than a compliment could be expected to—

Ho visto a 'l pianto mio
Risponder per pietate i sassi e l'onde,
E sospirar le fronde
Ho visto a 'l pianto mio;
Ma non ho visto mai
Né spero di vedere
Compassïon ne la crudele e bella,
Che non so s' io mi chiami o donna o fera;
Ma niega d'esser donna,
Poi che niega pietate
A chi non la negaro
Le cose inanimate.

(I. ii. 246–57)

At my laments I'ue heard the rocks, the waters
For pitty answer; and at my complaint
The leau'de boughes murmur, as they grieu'd for me;
But neuer saw, nor euer hope to see
Pitty in the faire and cruell (shall I say
Woman or) tygar? for a woman shee
Denyes to be, in thus denying me
The pitty this my miserable state
Drawes from things sencelesse, and inanimate.

(Sig. B_3)

There is much more here than extravagance, and the likening of the love of humans to the love of a vine for a tree is not meant as a simply illustrative figure of speech, but as a fact, a statement of the commonness of life everywhere. The same equivalence of belief and sensuality is part of the explanation of the beauty of those lines in which Aminta tells how he and Silvia grew up together, and where their companionship, not merely in retrospect, was, so to speak, instinctive:

Essendo io fanciulletto, sì che a pena
Giunger potea con la man pargoletta
A côrre i frutti da i piegati rami
De gli arboscelli, intrinseco divenni
De la più vaga e cara verginella
Che mai spiegasse al vento chioma d'oro.
La figliuola conosci di Cidippe
E di Montan, ricchissimo d'armenti,
Silvia onor de le selve, ardor de l'alme?
Di questa parlo, ahi lasso! Vissi a questa
Così unito alcun tempo, che fra due
Tortorelle più fida compagnia
Non sarà mai né fue.
Congiunti eran gli alberghi,
Ma più congiunti i cori:
Conforme era l'etate,
Ma 'l pensier più conforme:
Seco tendeva insidie con le reti
A i pesci ed a gli augelli, e seguitava
I cervi seco e le veloci damme;
E 'l diletto e la preda era comune.

(I. ii. 309–29)

Being but a Lad, so young as yet scarse able
To reach the fruit from the low-hanging boughes
Of new-growne trees; Inward I grew to bee
With a young mayde, fullest of loue and sweetnesse,
That ere display'd pure gold tresse to the winde;
Thou know'st her mother hight Cidippe; no?
Montano the rich Goteheard is her father:

Siluia, faire Siluia 'tis I meane, the glory
Of all these woods, and flame of euery heart;
'Tis shee, 'tis she I speake of; long alas
Liu'd I so neare her, and then lou'de of her,
As like two turtles each in other joy'de;
Neere our abodes, and neerer were our hearts;
Well did our yeares agree, better our thoughts;
Together woue we netts t'intrapp the fish
In flouds and sedgy fleetes; together sett
Pitfall for birds; together the pye'd Buck
And flying Doe ouer the plaines we chac'de;
And in the quarry', as in the pleasure shar'de.

(Sig. B_4)

The plot, for all its extravagance, is true to the strength and deviousness of the passion that rules nature:

Veramente la legge con che Amore
Il suo imperio governa eternamente
Non è dura né obliqua; e l'opre sue,
Piene di provvidenza e di misterio,
Altri a torto condanna.

(V. i. 1–5)

Doubtlesse the lawes wherewith *Loue* gouerneth
His Empire euermore, are neither hard
To follow, nor vniust; and those his workes
Which many men do condemne wrongfully,
Are full of prouidence, and mistery.

(Sig. I)

And although the resolution is happy (Silvia did not fall to the wolves, Aminta's leap did him little harm, and the two are finally brought together—all this proving indeed that love is inspired of Providence), the great power of the poem also depends on its insistence on the intricacy and bloodiness of desire. This is the poem's great achievement, the balance that gives each word its special power, where both obscenity and the virtue of innocence are given as the elements of passion. Where only conscience distinguishes men from animals, men can know, animals as they are, how love has ennobled them. So Love himself speaks—

e ben parrassi
Che la mia deità sia qui presente
In sé medesma e non ne' suoi ministri.
Spirerò nobil sensi a' rozzi petti,
Raddolcirò de le lor lingue il suono,
Perché, ovunque i' mi sia, io sono Amore,
Ne' pastori non men che ne gli eroi,
E la disagguaglianza de' soggetti,
Come a me piace, agguaglio. E questa è pure
Suprema gloria e gran miracol mio,
Render simìli a le più dotte cetre
Le rustiche sampogne. (*Prologo*, 77–88)

My godhead heere shall in it selfe appeare
Present no longer in my Ministers:
I'le breath soft thoughts into their courser brests,
And make their tungs in smoothest nũbers moue;
For wheresoere I am, still am I *Loue*;
No lesse in Shepherds then in greatest Peeres;
And inequallity in people, I
Can temper as I please, such is my power.
The Rurall sound of homely Shepherds reede
I can make equall with the learned'st lyre.
(Sig. A_3)

The values of love are clear to see,

Ché, sol amando, uom sa che sia diletto.
(II. ii. 223)

For only' a louers is the happy life.
(Sig. E_3)

The pains of love are fierce,

E pur fa tanto grandi e sì mortali
E così immedicabili le piaghe.
(II. i. 9–10)

[it] makes so deepe,
So deadly and immedicable wounds.
(Sig. D_3)

But when love is returned, all pain vanishes, all the trouble of lust is pardoned, and there is confidence—

egli conduce
L'uomo ad esser beato. (V. i. 6–7)

he leades
His votaries vnto their happiness.
(Sig. I)

When two such as Aminta and Silvia are moved to love each other it can be said,

Pari è l'età, la gentilezza è pari
E concorde il desío.
(V. i. 49–50)

Their age, their bloud and birth, their mutuall loues,
And all agree.
(Sig. I_2)

As it would have been in the Golden Age.

Such a view of love is dependent on the pastoral conception of the poem. We remember that the God of Love at the very beginning, in the style of the prologues of Euripides, had taken on the dress of a shepherd:

Chi crederia che sotto umane forme
E sotto queste pastorali spoglie
Fosse nascosto un Dio? non mica un Dio
Selvaggio, o de la plebe de gli Dei,
Ma tra' grandi e celesti il più potente,
Che fa spesso cader di mano a Marte
La sanguinosa spada, ed a Nettuno,
Scotitor de la terra, il gran tridente,
E le folgori eterne al sommo Giove.
(*Prologo*, 1–9)

Who would beleeue that in this human
    forme,
And vnder these meane Shepherds weedes,
A godhead? nor yet of the lower ranke,
But the most mighty 'mong the gods; whose
    powre
Makes oft the bloudy Sword of angry *Mars*
Fall from his hand; sterne *Neptune* hurle away
His powerfull trident, and great *Ioue* lay by
His thunderbolt.

(Sig. A_2)

It is part of his simple happiness to be without honour, the primeval state itself:

O bella età de l'oro,
Non già perché di latte
Se 'n corse il fiume e stillò mèle il bosco;
Non perché i frutti loro
Diêr da l'aratro intatte
Le terre, e gli angui errâr senz'ira o tòsco;
Non perché nuvol fosco
Non spiegò allor suo velo,
Ma in primavera eterna,
Ch'ora s'accende e verna,
Rise di luce e di sereno il cielo;
Né portò peregrino
O merce o guerra a gli altrui lidi il pino.
  Ma sol perché quel vano
Nome senza soggetto,
Quell' idolo d'errori, idol d' inganno,
Quel che da 'l volgo insano
Onor poscia fu detto,
Che di nostra natura il feo tiranno,
Non mischiava il suo affanno
Fra le liete dolcezze
De l'amoroso gregge;

Né fu sua dura legge
Nota a quell'alme in libertate avvezze;
Ma legge aurea e felice
Che Natura scolpì; *S' ei piace, ei lice.*
(I. ii. 570–95)

O Happy Age of Gould; happy' houres;
Not for with milke the riuers ranne,
And hunny dropt from eu'ry tree;
Nor that the Earth bore fruits, and flowres,
Without the toyle or care of Man,
And Serpents were from poyson free;
  Nor for th' Ayre (euer calme to see)
Had quite exil'de the lowring Night;
Whilst clad in an eternall Spring
(Now fiery hott, or else freezing)
The cheekes of heau'n smil'de with cleare light;
Nor that the wandring Pine of yore
Brought neither warres, nor wares from forraine shore;
  But therefore only happy Dayes,
Because that vaine and ydle name,
That couz'ning Idoll of vnrest,
(Whom the madde vulgar first did raize,
And call'd it *Honour*, whence it came
To tyrannize or'e eu'ry brest,)
  Was then suffred to molest
Poore louers hearts with new debate;
More happy they, by these his hard
And cruell lawes, were not debar'd
Their innate freedome; happy state;
The goulden lawes of Nature, they
Found in their brests; and then they did obey.
(Sig. D_1–D_2)

The doctrine includes the rejection of philosophy:

  Amore, in quale scola,
Da qual mastro s'apprende
La tua sì lunga e dubbia arte d'amare?

Chi n' insegna a spiegare
Ciò che la mente intende,
Mentre con l'ali tue sovra il ciel vola?
Non già la dotta Atene
Non Liceo ne 'l dimostra,
Non Febo in Elicona,
Che sì d'Amor ragiona
Come colà s' impara:
Freddo ne parla, e poco;
Non ha voce di foco,
Come a te si conviene;
Non alza i suoi pensieri
A par de' tuoi misteri.
Amor, degno maestro
Sol tu sei di te stesso,
E sol tu sei da te medesmo espresso.

(II. iii. 417–35)

O Loue, of whom, and where is taught
This thy so doubtfull Arte, and long
Of louing, that instructs the tounge
At ease to vtter eu'ry thought.
That the wilde fant'sie doth deuize?
Whilst with thy wings aboue the heau'n it flyes.
  The learned *Athens* taught it not;
Nor was it to *Liceus* knowne;
Apollo, god of *Helicon*
For all his knowledge knew it not.
Faint and cold is what he speakes,
Nor from his voice such a fire breakes
As doth thy greatnesse (Loue) befitt:
  Nor can his witt,
Or thoughts vnto the height arise
Of thy profounder misteries:
Thou readst thine owne lesson best
(Great *Loue*) and onely' art by thy selfe exprest.

(Sig. F_3–F_4)

Donadoni is right, of course, this makes Platonic love and its language a lie, and the innocence of the pastoral paradise is translated into a bacchanal[1]—this the very drunkenness of the senses blessed with the thought of fulfilment.

The *Aminta* turned out to be one of the great germinal poems of modern literature, the movement of its language so perfect and persuasive, its special harmony evidently presenting a whole range of experience to be thought about again and again and demanding to be exhausted. This germinal power, this demand to be carried on into other works of the imagination, comes from a balance Donadoni does not praise enough. It is a state of mind I think Tasso was the first to create for modern poetry, where the passion of love was known as cruel and insane and also innocent, and where it is understood that the power of its furious contradictions was the sign of its divinity: All such terms as these in speaking of Tasso must be taken in their strictest meanings—cruelty, insanity, divinity, innocence. In the full acceptance of pain and the terror of lust and cruelty Tasso continues to praise the divinity of the conscienceless son of Venus—

gli umani ingegni
Tu placidi ne rendi, e l'odio interno
Sgombri, Signor, da' mansüeti cori,
Sgombri mille furori;
E quasi fai co' l tuo valor superno
De le cose mortali un giro eterno.
(IV. ii. 355–60)

Thou smooth'st the rugged hearts of men;
And inward rancors driu'st away
(Great prince of happy peace;) and when
Milde breasts are troubled, do'st allay
Their woes; and by thy working strange,
Framst of things mortall, an eternall change.
(Sig. I)

The idea of the divinity of love, presented by a mind so

[1] *Torquato Tasso*, pp. 122–24, especially.

perceptive of all scepticism, so knowledgeable of all the arguments against the divinity of anything, is emphasized, perhaps even occasioned by the pain caused by the deprivation of love, and by the cruelty of scorn:

Non so se il molto amaro
Che provato ha costui servendo, amando,
Piangendo e disperando,
Raddolcito esser puote pienamente
D'alcun dolce presente.
Ma, se più caro viene
E più si gusta dopo 'l male il bene,
Io non ti chieggio, Amore,
Questa bëatitudine maggiore.

(V. i. 140–8)

I know not whether the much sowre
This (now blest) Louer (seruing, burning,
Now dispairing, and still mourning)
Hath felt; may in one happy' houre
Be thoroughly repay'd againe
With pleasure equall to his paine.
But if the good more pleasing be,
And come more welcome after wee
Haue felt the ill; I doe not craue
(O *Loue*) this happiness to haue.

(Sig. K_2)

Shakespeare's 116th sonnet makes no pastoral qualifications, claiming no more than the power of love over the finite world of history. But the idea of the age of gold and all the religiousness attached to that is necessary for Tasso in his astonishing effort to show how lust and cruelty can rule men as they do and in lives which know the beatitude of being loved:

Non bisogna la morte:
Ché a stringer core a core
Bastò prima la fede e poi l'amore.

Né quella che si cerca
È sì difficil fama,
Seguendo chi ben ama:
Ché amore è merce, e con amar si merca;
E cercando l'amor si trova spesso
Gloria immortale appresso.
(III. ii. 288–96)

Death, there is no neede of thee:
Loue alone, and Constancie
Ar enough (without thy Dart)
To tyre vpon an honest heart.
Yet so hard is not the way
To loues fame, as many say;
For Loue no price but loue regards;
And with it selfe, it selfe rewards.
And oft in seeking it, is found
Glory that liues, when we are vnder ground.
(Sig. H)

And if hell is, as for the Troubadour poets,[8] the mind of the lover whose love is not returned, Tasso kept expressing faith in the ways in which it might, or must be returned, the faith that divinity can never be denied, that it will work itself out in mysterious ways—

Oh con quant'arte
E per che ignote strade egli conduce
L'uomo ad esser beato, e fra le gioie
De 'l suo amoroso paradiso il pone,
Quando ei più crede a 'l fondo esser de' mali!
(V. i. 5–9)

And by how many vnknowne waies, he leades
His votaries vnto their happiness;
And placeth them among the highest ioyes
And pleasures of his amorous Paradise.
(Sig. I_2)

This is his way of balancing the fury of passion and its "beatitude," a risky one, but applicable to so much of experience as Guarini and a thousand others after him testify. It remained for Racine to destroy the idea, to show that such faith is for all its interest mad, and that the divinity raging in us will finally authorize the vile.

What is peculiar in the opening of the *Gerusalemme Liberata* is that it says nothing about love—

> Canto l'arme pietose e 'l capitano
> Che 'l gran sepolcro liberò di Cristo—[1]
>
> The sacred armies and the godly knight
> That the great sepulchre of Christ did free—[2]

when that plays so important a part in the management of the whole of the poem.

There are three love affairs in particular that are important, but except as the circumstances of one of them accounts for Rinaldo's long absence from the siege of Jerusalem their incidents are of no special consequence to the conduct of the Crusade. That is, this would still have been a poem about a successful Crusade had the love affairs been omitted although they serve, apart from their own interest, to acquaint us with the character of many important figures in a specially illuminating way. Seeing these persons in love helps us understand something about them as men and women living under strains still more dangerous than those of hardship, fatigue, drought, and the race for honour, and it helps us understand something of the confusion where some

> d'onore
> Fingon desio quel ch' è desio d'amore.
> (V. vii.)
>
> Call that knighthood which was childish love.

[1] From *Poesie*, ed. Francesco Flora, Milan: Rizzoli, 1934.

[2] *Godfrey of Bulloigne; Or The Recovery of Jerusalem*, tr. Edward Fairfax, 2 vols., New York, 1845–6.

On some occasions it has seemed advisable to use my own literal translation rather than Fairfax's, and in these instances the translated part is enclosed in brackets.

At times the excitement of the stories of passion equals and surpasses our interest in the Crusade itself. More than that, once or twice love seems to possess a higher value for the poet than the Christian religion, although Christian feeling is never absent from the verse even in the most powerful praise of sensuality.

It seems, indeed, that the beginning lines and the invocation do not fairly describe the poem's subject. If they did the *Gerusalemme Liberata* would probably be more nearly another kind of epic, and like Achilles Godfrey would be the clue to every action. As it is he is a great general, a great man, and rather apart from much of the poem. We know him quickly and after the first cantos there seems little more to know. But with Achilles we always learn more and finally he becomes the image of the world.

The central subject of this poem is something else, something that tells about the blindness of the human heart, the inscrutable will of things, inscrutable to man but known to God in all its secret ways. The very substance of this blindness in man and the pain around it is in this prayer—

amiamo or quando
Esser si puote rïamato amando.
(XVI. xv)

[Loving, may we be lov'd, embracing, be embrac'd.]

Love is happy only through God's choice and blessing. Without the grace of God love is a catastrophe. There are only two fortunate couples in the poem, the happy warrior and his bride, who are not fully presented, and the other, a shepherd and his wife living far away from war and courts—and God had given the shepherd's wife a will harmonious with her husband's:

l'antica moglie,
Che di conforme cor gli ha data il Cielo.
(VII. xvii)

[his aged wife
Whom Heaven had given a heart like his.]

But for such rare evidence of peace the poem is about the torment of the world, and that beginning epic couplet sounds empty. The poem never achieves the detachment and serenity those lines promise, although beside the sympathy and lyricism and melodrama there is much cool-headedness in the description of these passions the poet himself so clearly feels. But for all the clarity of Tasso's intellect, so true to itself and he so true to what he feels, there can never be anything like detachment to say nothing of serenity; and not for the usual reasons but because Tasso knows no other answers to the great question than those the figures in his poem know. It is one of the great triumphs of the poem, however, that the verse, the poet's lyricism expresses some of the same generosity his great heroes possess.

The integrity of the *Gerusalemme Liberata* thus depends on the relations of love and religion, and not of love and honour. For Spenser as for Homer and Ariosto the interest in glory takes no second place—each hero is "with child of glorious great intent," and the glory of the knight is the shadow of the glory of God. In Tasso there is no nationalism or patriotism, nothing in this poem about non-Italians to fortify any interest he might have in honour as a major subject.

When there are conflicts of love and honour among the Christians, the intensity of the struggle is usually reduced by the fortunate solution of removing the need for the final, terrible choice: both Rinaldo and Tancred retain honour and gain love. The story of Antony and Cleopatra is mentioned twice, and once, it seems, Tasso tries to lessen the tragedy of that story in excusing Antony from the criticism of cowardice. Tancred, who has an appointment to meet a Pagan in combat, wanders off, gets lost, and thus breaks his word to meet him at the appointed time—but however his absence was interpreted there was here no flight from honour for the sake of love. The single figure in the poem, I believe, who has this question to face and who makes his choice, is Altamor, an infidel, and for the sake of love he betrays honour (XX. lxix). And if this conventional conflict is thus unimportant to the poem, it is that much more clear that the integration depends on the harmony of the religious and romantic interests.[1]

The Crusade is, of course, the simple frame of the poem. The story, too, is simple, of the besiegers and the besieged, of reinforcements from earth and heaven and hell, a city captured, a counter-attack repulsed. In the matter of the siege itself one never ceases to be interested in Rinaldo's or Tancred's return to the attack, for this is the kind of action that demands a conclusion, and till a conclusion is in sight there must be suspense. And we know there will be a conclusion, the battle cannot last forever, somebody must win.

In this possibility of an end the military story plays its dominant part in the narrative however the love stories may interest us

[1] In this harmony Tasso succeeds in a miraculous way, but only if we grant the power of his religious expression: denying that we make of the poem a shambles. This it seems most critics have done, even great critics, but to this writer it seems that in general Carducci is certainly right: "Egli è l' erede legittimo di Dante Alighieri: crede e ragiona la sua fede per filosofia: ama, e comenta gli amori dottrinalmente: è artista, e scrive dialoghi di speculazioni scolastiche che vorrebbon esser platonici: innova, e teorizza. E come Dante, ha sempre qualcosa da rimproverarsi nella conscienza sua di cattolico: al suo poema pur essenzialmente religioso e cavalleresco, sovraintesse un' allegoria spirituale e morale: a ogni modo teme sempre di averlo fatto soverchiamente profano, e lo rifà purificato: né anche del rifacimento si contenta, e finisce co 'l poema della creazione. Egli è il solo cristiano del nostro Rinascimento. . . ." ("Dello Svolgimento della Letteratura Nazionale," in *Prose di Giosue Carducci*, MDCCCLIX—MCMIII, Bologna, 1905, p. 405.)

Fubini's remarks are also pertinent here: "Così la passione dei personaggi tasseschi viene ad avere una risonanza cosmica: tanto più profondamente serio, e sostanzialmente religioso ci sembra lo squardo del poeta che la contempla. E in realtà un sentimento così vivo, e sempre presente, del dolore e dei limiti dell' uomo non può non essere fondamentalmente religioso: né la religione della *Gerusalemme* è soltanto un elemento estraneo, introdotto in ossequio allo spirito del tempo, bensì un elemento essenziale della sua poesia. Sorge infatti, come sappiamo, da quella stessa dolorosa coscienza dei limiti umani (o meglio è una cosa sola con essa), il presentimento di un potere superiore che ci trascende e da cui siamo dominati: come dal travaglio della passione e della lotta sorge l'aspirazione a un mondo di purezza e di pace, in cui l'animo finalmente si acqueti." (Mario Fubini, *Studi sulla Letteratura del Rinascimento*, Florence: Sansoni, 1947, p. 310.)

otherwise, for love affairs need not have conclusions. Some cannot, perhaps, Tancred's and Clorinda's, Erminia's and Tancred's—the poem can give us no final fulfilment for these. So it is that the decision we look for in the battle has its special predominance in the interest of the narrative. And because the fighting is so vivid, the tension so great, the decision we look for carries a burden of significance we despair of finding in stories about the conclusion of this or that one's passion.

Yet the vividness of the passions of these stupendous men and women can make us forget the major circumstances of the poem no matter what suspense goes with them. There is, for example, the scene where Tancred recognizes Clorinda when she is dying: the journey to Armida's garden where she has Rinaldo under her power; in fact almost every scene of Armida's where she is raging at Rinaldo; when Tancred falls in love with Clorinda and even while the battle is fierce he draws her aside and at the risk of doing immense damage to the Christian war (and to our sympathy) offers to be her slave:

> Ecco io chino le braccia, e t'appresento
> Senza difesa il petto: or che no 'l fiedi?
> Vuoi ch'agevoli l'opra? i' son contento
> Trarmi l'usbergo or or, se nudo il chiedi.
>
> (III. xxviii)

> Save with thy grace, or let thine anger kill,
> Love hath disarm'd my life of all defence;
> An easy labor harmless blood to spill,
> Strike then, and punish where is none offence.

Only a sudden breaking of the battle about them prevented her taking him at his word.

But admitting the remarkable interruptions and the full power of the scene in Armida's Garden one can never forget that all this is in the midst of another hell; there is such constancy in Tasso's faith, such intensity in that religion of his, that even when his doctrine threatens to get lost while he relates the fatality of passion, he cannot possibly fail to remain true to the faith by whose light he sees everything. His very factuality is religious, and the whole poem is told with that same sense of sacred truth as in the story the Eunuch tells of the Angel who appeared to him in his dream:

> Vidi in sogno un guerrier, che minacciando
> A me su 'l volto il ferro ignudo pose.
> Imperïoso disse:—Io ti comando
> Ciò che la madre sua primier t' impose,
> Che battezzi l' infante: ella è diletta
> Del Cielo; e la sua cura a me s'aspetta.
>
> Io la guardo e difendo; io spirto diedi
> Di pietate a le fère, e mente a l'acque.
> (XII. xxxvi–xxxvii)

> I saw a champion clad in armor bright,
> That o'er my head shaked a flaming blade:
> He said—I charge thee execute aright
> That charge this infant's mother on thee laid;
> Baptize the child, high Heav'n esteems her dear,
> And I her keeper will attend her near:
>
> I will her keep, defend, save, and protect;
> I made the waters mild, the tigress tame.

That factuality of Tasso's, which brings with it so much of the surprise and delight of truth, is its own religiousness, and still somehow part of his Christianity. The Eunuch goes on to say, as he thinks of the circumstances that kept him from seeing to Clorinda's baptism, thinking too of his own religion—

> Or odi dunque tu, che 'l Ciel minaccia
> A te, diletta mia, strani accidenti.
> Io non so; forse a lui vien che dispiaccia
> Ch'altri impugni la fé de' suoi parenti.
> Forse è la vera fede. (XII. xl)

> Hear then, my joy, my hope, my darling, hear!
> High heav'n some dire misfortune threatened hath,
> Displeas'd, pardie, because I did thee lear
> A lore repugnant to thy parents' faith.
> [Perhaps it is the true faith.]

Forse è la vera fede! so passionate a regard for truth, so sure a restraint, neither damning nor praising the man. Like Ariosto Tasso grants the Saracens all the capacities of humanity.

In the matters of love, too, he sees as plainly as here the holiness of the fact prevailing:

> Fu stupor, fu vaghezza, e fu diletto
> S'amor non fu, che mosse il cor villano.
>
> (II. xxi)

> It was amazement, wonder and delight,
> Although not love, that moved his cruel sense.

And so with war. The crusades may have been noble to him but war was horror, as horrible as for Ariosto, and as for the Soldan looking on at the battle:

> Or, mentre in guisa tal fèra tenzone
> É tra 'l fedel essercito e 'l pagano,
> Salse in cima a la torre ad un balcone,
> E mirò, ben che lunge, il fèr Soldano:
> Mirò, quasi in teatro od in agone,
> L'aspra tragedia de lo stato umano,
> I vari assalti, e il fèro orror di morte,
> E i gran giochi del caso e de la sorte.
>
> Stette attonito alquanto e stupefatto
> A quelle prime viste. . . .
>
> (XX. lxxiii–lxxiv)

> Between the armies twain while thus the fight
> Wax'd sharp, hot, cruel, though renew'd but late,
> The Soldan climb'd up to the tower's height,
> And saw far off their strife and fell debate;
> As from some stage or theatre, the knight
> Saw play'd the tragedy of human state,
> Saw death, blood, murder, wo and horror strange,
> And the great acts of fortune, chance and change.
>
> At first astonish'd and amaz'd he stood,
> Then burnt with wrath, and self-consuming ire. . . .

Perhaps it is only to the degree that we value this truthfulness of Tasso's that we are able to judge his analysis of the nature of love, accepting it as an analysis as well as a celebration. Only as we understand a kind of studious intentness in this are we able to discover the relation of love and religion in the conception of the whole work. But if we are so persuaded, this, however ironic, becomes a key passage:

> Qual meraviglia or fia, s' il fèro Achille
> D'Amor fu preda, ed Ercole e Teseo,
> S'ancor chi per Giesú la spada cinge,
> L'empio ne' lacci suoi talora stringe?
>
> (IV. xcvi)

> What wonder if Achilles were misled,
> Or great Alcides, at their ladies' sights,
> Since these true champions of the Lord Above
> Were thralls to beauty, yielden slaves to love?

If at one moment one might be the servant of love, at another of Christ, then one can believe that the chief evil of love is adventitious, in the interruptions it demands from duty, even from religious oaths. Armida can overpower even the sworn soldiers of Jesus. When Rinaldo wastes his time with her and gets soft, he looks in the mirror and finds that sensuality has distorted him and taken away his character as a soldier, almost as a man. In the extreme, sensuality, as an accompaniment of love, destroys the manly character. And this, I take it, is why it is Rinaldo who must overcome the forces of sensuality, the forest, for only the most heroic man of all the Christians is able to destroy its power.

What such strength overcomes is but for its distraction good. The illustrations of this are marvellous in their beauty. There is the passage when two warriors who have been sent out to rescue Rinaldo from Armida on the magic mountain come across Sirens who try to keep them from continuing on their way, and in describing the beauty of one of these Tasso searched for similes:

Qual matutina stella da l'onde
Rugiadosa e stillante; o come fuore
Spuntò, nascendo giá da le feconde
Spume de l'oceán, la dea d'amore.

(XV. lx)

As when the morning star escap'd and fled
From greedy waves with dewy beams up flies,
Or as the queen of love, new born and bred
Of th' ocean's fruitful froth, did first arise.

Qual matutina stella! And at the other extreme there is the description of the embrace of Rinaldo and Armida, the simple power of passion. (XVI. 18–19.) And again, the only evil here would have been an interruption to duty, for in deserting her Rinaldo honestly offers to continue to be her cavalier:

Sarò tuo cavalier, quanto concede
La guèrra d'Asia e con l'onor la fede.

(XVI. liv)

Call me your soldier and your knight, as far
As Christian faith permits and Asia's war.

(XVI. liii)

There is perhaps another evil inevitable to love, its inextinguishableness, "de l'amor la sete" (VI. cx). Sovereign from its first incursion—

Oh maraviglia! Amor, ch'a pena è nato,
Giá grande vola, e giá trïonfa armato—

(I. xlvii)

O love, O wonder; love new born, new bred,
Now grown, now arm'd, this champion captive led—

it threatens to take over the lives of its victims for the rest of their days, and all their thought, and Tasso will use the same figures of speech to describe the power of this love that he will use for religion—

or godi, e pasci
In Dio gli occhi bramosi, o felice alma;
Ed hai del bene oprar corona e palma. (III. lxviii)

now feed thine eyes
With thy Redeemer's sight, where crown'd with bliss
Thy faith, zeal, merit, well deserving is.

This vast and terrible power deserves the same terms because it too is divine, it is immortal, lasting beyond death and becoming part of the divine love. This we understand plainly when the ghost of Clorinda appears to Tancred in a dream:

Ed ecco, in sogno, di stellata veste
Cinta gli appar la sospirata amica:
Bella assai piú; ma lo splendor celeste
Orna, e non toglie la notizia antica:
E con dolce atto di pietá le meste
Luci par che gli asciughi, e cosí dica:
—Mira come son bella e come lieta,
Fedel mio caro; e in me tuo duolo acqueta.

Tale io son, tua mercé: tu me da i vivi
Del mortal mondo, per error, togliesti;
Tu in grembo a Dio fra gl' immortali e divi,
Per pietá, di salir degna mi fêsti.
Quivi io beata amando godo, e quivi
Spero che per te loco anco s'appresti,
Ove al gran sole e ne l'eterno die
Vagheggiarai le sue bellezze e mie.

Se tu medesmo non t' invidii il Cielo,
E non travii co 'l vaneggiar de' sensi,
Vivi, e sappi ch' io t'amo, e non te 'l celo,
Quanto piú creatura amar conviensi.—
Cosí dicendo, fiammeggio di zelo
Per gli occhi, fuor del mortal uso accensi;
Poi nel profondo de' suoi rai si chiuse,
E sparve, e novo in lui conforto infuse.

(XII. xci–xciii)

And clad in starry veil, amid his dream
  (For whose sweet sake he mourn'd) appear'd the maid,
Fairer than erst, yet with that heav'nly beam,
  Not out of knowledge was her lovely shade;
With looks of ruth her eyes celestial seem
  To pity his sad plight, and thus she said:—
Behold how fair, how glad thy love appears,
And for my sake, my dear, forbear these tears:

Thine be the thanks, my soul thou madest flit
  At unawares out of her earthly nest;
Thine be the thanks, thou hast advanced it
  In Abraham's dear bosom long to rest;
There still I love thee, there for Tancred fit
  A seat prepared is among the bless'd;
There in eternal joy, eternal light,
Thou shalt thy love enjoy, and she her knight;

Unless thyself thyself heav'n's joys envy,
  And thy vain sorrow thee of bliss deprive:
Live; know I love thee, that I nill deny,
  As angels men, as saints may wights alive.—
This said, of zeal and love forth of her eye
  A hundred glorious beams bright shining drive,
Amid which rays herself she clos'd from sight,
And with new joy, new comfort, left her knight.

I think Tasso means to say that in the conduct of their love affairs men may be as guilty of crimes and foolishness as in the conduct of Crusades, that human life is always in confusion, but just as the life of a follower of Christ has its authority in God, so does the life of love. For it is only with some such notion that he could hope to rescue these heroes and heroines of his from madness, and what is perhaps even more terrible from the sanity that tells them they no longer have the power of direction over themselves. There is nothing either Tancred or Erminia or Armida can do to change or divert or kill their loves. They are powerless finally, and Armida in her twistings and her rages, her flights and attempts at suicide, is the final proof of this, she who till her own possession was the most brilliant and conscienceless of magicians, glorying in her power—

> L'uno di servitú, l'altra d' impero
> Si gloria, ella in se stessa, ed egli in lei.
>
> (XVI. xxi)

> Her to command, to serve it pleas'd the knight;
> He proud of bondage, of her empire she.

She became perfectly subjected to the power she once asserted. Passion leads to every extreme, even treason. Tancred is almost ready to betray his religion. In Ariosto, too, there is something of the view of love as a blind and invincible power, but there in its raging it seems a merely human madness. But almost any character of Tasso's is more wildly possessed than even Orlando, driven in hidden and mysterious ways—

> Temerò me medesmo, e, da me stesso
> Sempre fuggendo, avrò me sempre a presso.
>
> (XII. lxxvii)

> Swift from myself I run, myself I fear,
> Yet still my hell within myself I bear.

Like Dido, or even Phèdre, with the astonishing difference that for the persons of this poem this apparently diabolical possession ultimately turns to good: Clorinda is baptized through love; Armida, we must suppose, is also brought to the true faith; and while Erminia can hardly hope to be more than a patient nurse, her misery is surely lessened. Such passionate possession apparently works in harmony with the will of God.

This idea, extraordinary in itself, determines the importance of chance in the universe of the poem, especially since the characters are given so little to philosophy. And there is no philosophic basis for morality, I think, expressed either by the writer or his characters, and no philosophic conception of love. To the degree that these images of passion are made vivid, common sense may be said to support this most powerful imagination—observation, and what one might call elementary inferences, but nothing like a theory, Platonic or materialist or whatever. So that the question is peculiarly urgent—how can it happen that this rage should work together with God? The answer seems to be only this—by coincidence. It is purely by chance that Tancred sees the warrior who has burned the Crusaders' tower and who turns out to be Clorinda; it is by chance that Erminia discovers what she takes to be the dead body of Tancred; it is by chance that Rinaldo reaches Armida before she kills herself and so comes to the reconciliation.

Coincidence does not always work to good, for it is by accident that Tancred causes Clorinda's death. But even this is no lasting disaster since I believe we are to understand that the fortune of these lovers before death is relatively unimportant. For the same accident leads to Clorinda's baptism and so to the felicity in eternity that she can promise, in Tancred's dream, for them both.

Love is a passion, then, an obsession, endangering even religion and certainly all other duties, but somehow dear to God, and so He in surely some meaningful way that appears to us only in the form of chance makes us know that this is as He would have it. It is this faith, then, that justifies us in our surrender to the rage, that justifies the ordinary human notion of the innocence of love. Somehow Tasso must give the contradiction its complete force, and so the sense of innocence comes again to his support. It is developed especially, perhaps, in the pastoral part of the poem, most noticeably in the description of Armida's garden. And where Spenser's Bower of Bliss and many another scene has as one of its qualities the beauty of something imagined, this somehow seems a real place, through that passionate factuality of Tasso's, full of the sense of the perfection of what you can see and touch and smell:

L'aura, non ch'altro, è de la maga effetto,
L'aura che rende gli alberi fioriti:
Co' fiori eterni eterno il frutto dura,
E mentre spunta l'un, l'altro matura.

Nel tronco istesso e tra l' istessa foglia
Sovra il nascente fico invecchia il fico:
Pendono a un ramo, un con dorata spoglia,
L'altro con verde, il novo e 'l pomo antico:

Lussureggiante serpe alto e germoglia
La tòrta vite ov' è più l'orto aprico:
Qui l'uva ha in fiori acerba, e qui d'òr l'have
E di piropo, e giá di nettar grave.

(XVI. x–xi)

Mild was the air, the skies were clear as glass,
  The trees no whirlwind felt nor tempest's smart,
But ere their fruit drop off the blossom comes;
This springs, that falls, that rip'neth, and this blooms.

The leaves upon the self-same bough did hide,
  Beside the young, the old and ripened fig;
Here fruit was green, there ripe with vermeil side,
  The apples new and old grew on one twig;
The fruitful vine her arms spread high and wide,
  That bended underneath their clusters big;
The grapes were tender here, hard, young and sour,
There purple, ripe, and nectar sweet forth pour.

In the wonderful song of the miraculous bird there is all the innocence of nature to serve man's enjoyment:

Cogliam la rosa in su 'l mattino adorno
Di questo dí, che tosto il seren perde;
Cogliam d'amor la rosa: amiamo or quando
Esser si puote rïamato amando.

(XVI. xv)

O gather then the rose while time thou has,
  Short is the day, done when it scant began,
Gather the rose of love while yet thou mayst,
Loving be lov'd, embracing be embrac'd.

The pastoral scenes in the sixth and seventh cantos are relatively brief scenes, with their own charm but without the sustainment of the Pastorella episode. They have the special charm of this same factuality, and we find, for example, that the old shepherd who has left the neighbourhood of the court for the quiet life of the country is not in the usual convention a retired courtier but a gardener (VII. 12). And these scenes are not meant to present perfection so much as places of temporary refuge and solace. This is Erminia's idea of Nature itself—

L' innamorata donna iva co 'l cielo
Le sue fiamme sfogando ad una ad una;
E secretarii del suo amore antico
Fea I muti campi e quel silenzio amico.

(VI. ciii)[1]

And Cinthia-like for beauty's glorious light,
The love-sick nymph threw glist'ring beams around;
And counsellors of her old love she made
Those valleys dumb, that silence, and that shade.

The Shepherd also thinks of Nature as a place of content—

O sia grazia del Ciel, che l'umiltade
D'innocente pastor salvi e sublime;
O che, sí come il folgore non cade
In basso pian ma su l'eccelse cime,
Cosí il furor di peregrine spade
Sol de' gran re l'altere teste opprime;
Né gli avidi soldati a preda alletta
La nostra povertá vile e negletta.

(VII. ix)

[1] Donadoni's comment is again penetrating: "Come già nel *Rinaldo*, il paesaggio apparisce nella *Gerusalemme* come artificiato: è il paessaggio veduto da un cortigiano; non è il prato, nè il colle, nè il bosco, nè la valle: è il giardino: il giardino di Armida (XVI), chiuso nel centro del tondo edificio, circondato da labirinti che lo rendono inaccessibile: lá parte riservata di un regio parco. È in quello tutto è bellezza di artificio, anche se

l'arte che tutto fa, nulla si scopre. . . .

Si confronti questo giardino con la reggia e gli orti di Alcina nel *Furioso*, e si avrà chiara la diversa se non pure opposta maniera, onde la Natura si presenta ai due poeti: all'uno in tutta la sua spontaneità e ricchezza: all'altro limitata e corretta da un meraviglioso maestro di giardinaggio." (*Torquato Tasso*, p. 193.)

Haply just heav'ns, defence and shield of right,
  Doth love the innocence of simple swains;
The thunderbolts on highest mountains light,
  And seld or never strike the lower plains;
So kings have cause to fear Bellona's might,
  Not they whose sweat and toil their dinner gains,
Nor ever greedy soldier was enticed
By poverty, neglected and despised.

Beyond such an emphasis the pastoral scenes convey contrasts and ideas not to be found in significant ways in Boiardo and Ariosto, although Boiardo has some interest in related ideas. Here the scenes of country peace are especially contrasted with war—

né strepito di Marte
Ancor turbò questa remota parte.
(VII. viii)

This wilderness doth us in safety keep,
No thund'ring drum, no trumpet breaks our sleep.

And here, too, there is a kind of reflection of humanity in the life of nature. It is strange that Tasso should show the bonds between the two in this way, and as usual there is nothing philosophical to explain the relation. It is none the less genuine and moving, and it suggests the one point at which we might suppose Tasso could conceive that the innocence of love derives from the innocence of nature. There is this simile, for instance, describing Erminia's flight:

  Si come cerva, ch'assetata il passo
Mova a cercar d'acque lucenti e vive,
Ove un bel fonte distillar d'un sasso,
O vide un fiume tra frondose rive,
Se incontra i cani allor che 'l corpo lasso
Ristorar crede a l'onde, a l'ombre estive,
Volge in dietro fuggendo, e la paura
La stanchezza obliar face e l'arsura;

Cosí costei, che de l'amor la sete,
Onde l'infermo core è sempre ardente,
Spegner ne l'accoglienze oneste e liete
Credeva, e riposar la stancha mente;
Or che contra le vien chi gliel diviete,
E 'l suon del ferro e le minaccie sente,
Se stessa e 'l suo desir prima abbandona,
E 'l veloce destrier timida sprona.

(VI. cix–cx)

As when a chased hind her course doth bend
To seek by soil to find some ease or good,
Whether from craggy rock the spring descend,
Or softly glide within the shady wood,
If there the dogs she meet where late she wend
To comfort her weak limbs in cooling flood,
Again she flies swift as she fled at first,
Forgetting weakness, weariness, and thirst:

So she, that thought to rest her weary spright,
And quench the endless thirst of ardent love,
With dear embracements of her lord and knight,
But such as marriage rites should first approve;
When she beheld her foe, with weapon bright,
Threat'ning her death, his hasty courser move,
Her love, her lord, herself abandoned,
She spurr'd her speedy steed, and swift she fled.

Suggestions like this are infrequent, for Tasso cannot think long of the pastoral without discovering a satyr there.[1]

It seems that the occasional pastoral parts, the faith in coincidence, the happy resolutions, perhaps beyond the grave, are part of the single conception of the innocence of love. Knowing what

[1] Carducci's generalization is important: "Il satiro è uno degli elementi necessari alla pastorale: amatore e persecutore selvaggio di ninfe, egli rappresenta la rozza sensualità primitiva di contro alla trasfigurazione dell' amore operata nella vita pastorale dalla poesia e dalla musica." ("Su l'Aminta di T. Tasso," in *Opera*, XIV (1944), 144.)

he does about passion, perhaps as much as Ariosto, unlike Ariosto he is asserting the difference between love and passion without love, the crucial difference for Tasso, and perhaps to be defined simply as that constancy in passion which God has brought about in conferring immortality.

Whatever the values shared by nature and humanity, or however we fix upon defining their identity, the *Gerusalemme Liberata* is a poem unified in conception, and in the true romantic way, which is to say all integrated in the passions and theories of the poet. The *Aminta* with its sense of perfection was expanded in this respect in the greater poem so that the religious interests of the poet could be known for what they were, that his whole nature might have its scope. Dondadoni, a severe critic of Tasso's failures of intellect and religion, is as always respectful of his power, and I believe he speaks justly when he compares the unity of this poem with that of the *Orlando Furioso*: "The unity of the *Gerusalemme Liberata* is a vision of the most disparate elements at a single instant, all brought together by a feeling fundamentally generative, by an enthusiasm that is always fiery and active. The unity of the *Furioso* is the product of pondering and calculation, a harmony of parts, and the dominance of thought over complex and formless matter. It is like that divine act that brings the universe out of chaos. The unity of the *Liberata* is in the constancy of the poet's sentiment and passion. And the various parts are connected with each other and with the whole, never or hardly ever from extrinsic causes, but from the very impetus with which the poet abandons himself in the characters and the situations."[1]

How much this passion of the poet controls things, matters even more than the presentation of passion itself, and how it leads to unity, all this is best seen in observing the relations of men with the supernatural. God and His angels, and the Devil and his followers, are, of course, personages who intervene rather

[1] *Torquato Tasso*, pp. 177–78.

Francesco Flora has commented that all Tasso's poetry is assimilated in the same lyric tone, "tutti concorrono ad una sintesi tonale in cui consiste l'originalità di un tanto poeta." ("Unità Lirica delle Opere Poetiche di Torquato Tasso," *Letterature Moderne*, III [1952], 389.)

frequently in the action of the poem. Their acts are as specific and even mechanical as if done by men, as we see when God's angels are building military defences or when Beelzebub makes a false Clorinda. These and other deeds are part of the war between the Devil and God, occasioned in the will of each, but after a while God commands the Devil to be still and to let the mortals continue their own battles without his interference. God's help at times is in answer to a prayer, and there are also the actions of magicians who obtain supernatural help in sending two warriors to rescue Rinaldo, or who enlist all Hell to enchant a forest.

In this mingling of the personages of earth and Hell and Heaven the geographical barriers are fairly clear; we visualize the scene clearly when we see, for example, the devils in their home beneath the earth, or the angel's long voyage from Heaven to the earth. These indications clearly establish the sense of separateness, and beyond themselves the systems of communication between these regions fit the traditional Christian notion of the way things go in the universe. At the same time, anything like a philosophical explanation is lacking, so that when the final struggle is carried on by men who must now depend only on their own efforts, one is moved to think that again Tasso is acting instinctively, and not as a philosopher. It is only in his rather coherent treatment of magic that one can judge the harmony of his feeling with traditional Christian attitudes, and to infer from this that his unspoken unabstracted thought agrees with Christian philosophy.[1] All that

[1] "L'eroico doveva differenziarsi dal romanzesco; ma non rinunciare ad uno dei mezzi che più avevano assicurato il successo dei romanzi. 'Poco dilettevole è veramente quel poema, che non ha seco quelle meraviglie, che tanto muovono non solo l'animo degli ignoranti, ma dei giudiziosi ancora: parlo di quelli anelli, di quelli scudi incantati, di quei corsieri volanti, di quelle navi converse in ninfe [bisognava, al teorizzatore dell'eroico, chiamar Virgilio a sostegno dell'Ariosto], di quelle larve, che tra i combattenti si tramettono, e d'altre cose sì fatte, delle quali, quasi di sapori, debbe giudizioso scrittore condire il suo poema.' (A. P., I.) E solo per omaggio ai censori, e con grande renitenza, il Tasso sopprimeva, dalla prima stesura della *Liberata*, più pagine di racconti magici e meravigliosi.

"Ma voleva essere un meraviglioso serio: un meraviglioso religioso, la cui

matters in the poem, however, is that there should be nothing in the magical or mythological actions to contradict the orthodox Christian scheme of things.

Even so, there is no such sharp separation of worlds as in Ariosto, for here the supernatural beings mingle much more frequently with men, the strength of religious feeling is so great and the uses of magic so pervasive that at any time one half expects the natural and the supernatural to change places. Yet there is not, of course, so close a linking of worlds as in some Neo-Platonic poems, or even as occasionally in Spenser when it is possible to apply the teaching that "soule is forme, and doth the bodie make." Tasso has no use for ideas to explain the interactions in his universe.

There is another factor also, I think, that causes Tasso to preserve the sense of the separateness of the realms of being, his notion of the misery of human life and the difficulty of seeing just how evil will turn to good through the sole help of chance:

causa, come si è detto, fossero Dio, o i demoni permessi da Dio. Di fronte al soprannaturale, il Tasso non conosce il sorriso del primo Rinascimento." (Donadoni, *Torquato Tasso*, p. 141.)

I am myself not sure that the remarks of Carmelo Previtera on the magic of the poem do not go farther than I can follow, but they help define the relation of the use of magic to the inspiration of the poem: "[In Armida] L'arte magica diviene movimento psicologico, raffinata esperienza del senso e del sentimento. L'addormentarsi di Rinaldo cullato dal canto melodioso di una Sirena, il viaggio del giovene eroe, avvinto da tenaci catene di fiori, su un carro volante, verso l'isola solitaria e incantata, il giardino di Armida con le sue vie tortuose, vario di mostri che atteriscono, di fontane misteriose, di ninfe seducenti, ricco d'immagini rappresentanti antiche storie d'amore, la dimora della maga dove sono accumulate meraviglie su meraviglie, e poi l'invocazione degli spiriti infernali, la distruzione del castello incantato e la fuga della maliarda sono tutti elementi—in ciò che non sia imitazione meccanica, materia tradizionale, artifizio rettorico ed ornamento decorativo—di uno stesso momento spirituale che genera i temi diversi: la passione amorosa con i suoi languori, le sue tristezze, i suoi fremiti, i suoi furori disperati. E perciò la poesia più che dal meraviglioso è generata dai motivi preferiti dal poeta: l'amore e il senso, due note dominanti su tutte le altre, come una voce musicale persistente, che ha larghi echi ed alte risonanze." (*La Poesia e l'Arte di Torquato Tasso*, Milan: Giuseppe Principato, 1936, p. 226.)

Mirò, quasi in teatro od in agone,
L'aspra tragedia de lo stato umano,
I vari assalti, e il fèro orror di morte,
E i gran giochi del caso e de la sorte.

(XX. lxxiii)

As from some stage or theatre, the knight
Saw play'd the tragedy of human state,
Saw death, blood, murder, wo and horror strange,
And the great acts of fortune, chance and change.

If we except Godfrey, and this may not be necessary, there is no one in the poem who is not on the edge of despair and destruction. Even the incidents from folklore become part of the mystery of pain: the story of the knight bearing his own cut-off head that talks, the lion that nurses the child, the men turned into beasts by a magician. And only the story of the lion keeps much of its child-like wonder, where some of the terror is merely imagined. In short, the poem also exploits the meaninglessness of experience, I suppose one could say the tragedy of pain. At any rate, experience so deep it justifies Tasso in his neglect of philosophy and in his use of faith.

Tasso is so passionately held by the idea of the supernatural that his imagination is led even into "Gothic" wildness, but that terrible enchanted wood, one of the most tremendous images in all poetry, cannot be thought of as allegorically conceived. Its power corresponds to nothing, I think, in the allegorical method of *La Queste del Saint Graal* or *The Faerie Queene* or *Pilgrim's Progress.* One can find nothing in it to reveal a system of thought or ethics, although as with the finest symbols and metaphors each detail in the scene seems full of meaning, changed and enriched at every view. If the wood has its obvious allegorical suggestions, as of the wilderness of the senses, no gloss can make it only that in a defined scheme, for one thing because for Tasso the senses and the good and evil they effect are only partly definable, and they are partly mysterious and divine.

In one way or another we know that the forest is the enemy of every Christian knight, perhaps of humanity, and we know that in some way it threatens a knight in the way a life of sensuality does, distracting and wasting his strength. Beyond such acknowledgments there is almost no comment we can make upon the forest in interpreting the dangers it presents.

When Godfrey finally sends Rinaldo to try his skill in subduing the horror that has endangered the efforts of all his forces, he speaks in this way:

> Quinci al bosco t' invia, dove cotanti
> Son fantasmi ingannevoli e bugiardi.
> Vincerai (questo so) móstri e giganti,
> Pur ch'altro folle error non ti ritardi.
> Deh! né voce che dolce or piango o canti,
> Né beltá che soave o rida o guardi,
> Con tenere lusinghe il cor ti pieghi;
> Ma sprezza i finti aspetti e i finti preghi.
>
> (XVIII. x)

> That done, march to the wood, whence each one brings
> Such news of furies, goblins, fiends and sprites:
> The giants, monsters, and all dreadful things
> Thou shalt subdue, which that dark grove unites;
> Let no strange voice that mourns or sweetly sings,
> Nor beauty whose glad smile frail hearts delights,
> Within thy breast make ruth or fury rise,
> But their false looks and prayers false despise.

There is not only music or tender weeping to confront:

> Dove in passando le vestigia ei posa,
> Par ch'ivi scaturisca, o che germoglie:
> Lá s'apre il giglio, e qui spunta la rosa;
> Qui sorge un fonte, ivi un ruscel si scioglie:
> E sovra e intorno a lui la selva annosa
> Tutte parea ringiovenir le foglie:
> S'ammolliscon le scorze, e si rinverde
> Piú lietamente in ogni pianta il verde.
>
> (XVIII. xxiii)

Whereso he stepp'd, it seem'd the joyful ground
  Renew'd the verdure of her flowery weed;
A fountain here, a well-spring there he found;
  Here bud the roses, there the lilies spreed;
The aged wood o'er and about him round
  Flourish'd with blossoms new, new leaves, new seed;
And on the boughs and branches of those treen
The bark was soften'd, and renew'd the green.

  Fermo il guerrier ne la gran piazza, affisa
A maggior novitate allor le ciglia.
Quercia gli appar, che per se stessa incisa
Apre feconda il cavo ventre, e figlia:
E n'esce fuor vestita in strana guisa
Ninfa d'etá cresciuta (oh meraviglia!);
E vede insieme poi cento altre piante
Cento Ninfe produr dal sen pregnante.

(XVIII. xxvi)

Upon the tree his eyes Rinaldo bent,
  And there a marvel great and strange began;
An aged oak beside him cleft and rent,
  And from his fertile hollow womb forth ran
(Clad in rare weeds and strange habiliment)
  A nymph for age able to go to man;
An hundred plants beside, even in his sight,
Childed an hundred nymphs, so great, so dight.

The Nymphs welcome him singing:

—Ben caro giungi in queste chiostre amene,
O de la donna nostra amore e spene.

  Giungi aspettato a dar salute a l'egra,
D'amoroso pensiero arsa e ferita.
Questa selva che dianzi era sí negra,
Stanza conforme a la dolente vita,
Vedi che tutta al tuo venir s'allegra,
E 'n piú leggiadre forme è rivestita.

(XVIII. xxviii–xxix)

Welcome, dear lord! welcome to this sweet grove;
Welcome, our lady's hope! welcome her love!

Thou com'st to cure our princess, faint and sick
For love; for love of thee, faint, sick, distressed;
Late black, late dreadful, was this forest thick,
Fit dwelling for sad folk with grief oppressed;
See, with thy coming how the branches quick
Revived are, and in new blossoms dressed.

Rinaldo resists them, and when he advances into the forest as if to attack it, as in a nightmare one might with weapons attack a forest, it turns into a creature like Briareus, a giant with a hundred arms, with fifty shields and fifty swords. Thunder and lightning race through the forest, the earth trembles, tempests rage, and Rinaldo only by being unterrified finally breaks the charm:

Tornò sereno il cielo e l'aura cheta;
Tornò la selva al natural suo stato;
Non d'incanti terribile, né lieta;
Piena d'orror, ma de l'orror innato.
Ritenta il vincitor s'altro piú vieta
Ch'esser non possa il bosco omai troncato;
Poscia sorride, e fra sé dice:—Oh vane
Sembianze! e folle chi per voi rimane!—
(XVIII. xxxviii)

The heav'ns grew clear, the air wax'd calm and still,
The wood returned to its wonted state;
Of witchcrafts free, quite void of spirits ill,
Of horror full, but horror there innate:
He further prov'd if aught withstood his will
To cut those trees as did the charms of late;
And finding naught to stop him, smil'd and said—
O shadows vain! O fools, of shades afraid!

De Sanctis' words on Tasso here are fine: "He even gives us an enchanted wood, that is, an artificial wood, a wood that exists for a reason outside of itself. In the romantic literature of chivalry enchantment, like Nature, was always arbitrary, was nothing but extraordinary combinations of appearances, which awaken curiosity and wonder. But magic, as Tasso shows it, is reasonable, we can understand it: it is Nature touched up by art and used for a definite end. His enchanted wood, like his enchanted garden and palace, is the work of an artist who poses it himself and for his own purposes. The conception of the enchanted wood is not new; it is the well-known wood of false appearances, the wood of error, of the passions. But the thing that is very original in Tasso is his treatment of it. The wood is himself in miniature, the whole of his world of elegy and idyll, condensed and emphasized. Erminia and Armida, Tancredi and Rinaldo, all of Tasso's creations and the whole of his poetic soul, are fused together in that wood—all that is tenderest in elegy, and all that is softest in the idyll, and in their notes of sweetest music."[1] So, with the gods everywhere and Hell emptied—

> Votò Pluton gli abissi—
>
> (IX. xv)
>
> [Pluto emptied the abysses!]—

the passionate faith excludes system, the supernatural is almost commonplace, and the only miracles are the miracles of chance, Tancred's recognizing Clorinda, Erminia's discovery of Tancred, the Egyptian king's arrival after the city has fallen. Erminia kisses the corpse, still by chance alive, and that too seems a miracle. Tancred in the terrible woods, not knowing what to do, strikes a tree, and that tree of all of them turns out to be Clorinda. Not the real one—that would have been a true miracle, but this was the false one, the one the fiends saw to it should appal him. But to Tancred it seemed a miracle that this should be she.

The truly miraculous has lost as much of its standing as if this had been an allegory. Miracles are most seriously regarded when the universe is known to be an order and they are interruptions in the order, but in Tasso's universe there is no order. Even the hierarchy of society can be subverted, and the Duke can fight as a private soldier, indeed feels morally compelled to. The pagan can be as noble as the Christian. The witch can become a saint. There

[1] Francesco De Sanctis, *History of Italian Literature*, tr. Joan Redfern, New York, 1931, pp. 662–63.

is no chain of being. The miraculous is the unexpected, the divine is the coincidence that turns out well, and Tasso's faith is unshakable—it will.

Generally in romances the end but continues the aspiration with which the story began, and even the account of Galahad's vision of the Grail includes the prayer for translation to the skies. So it is in much of the *Liberata*, the recovery of Jerusalem is but one step in Godfrey's pilgrimage, the thirst for heaven is still insatiable. The satisfaction of some of the lovers is likewise incomplete. But in the enchanted forest Rinaldo remains in command of himself and defeats the wilderness. Here the great climax is not in a seeking but in a demonstration, and it is the clue I think to the quality in the *Liberata* that transcends the romantic wonder in creating another kind, the wonder of faith rather than of aspiration. The *roman educatif* of *Rinaldo* and of so much of the other romantic writing had been left behind, even the identification of the narrator with the questing hero was put aside, and Rinaldo acted as a man in control of his own life, in the self-sufficiency of a Homeric or a Shakespearean character. There is much other characterization of the same order in the *Liberata*, and one may speak of it as epic or dramatic in Ker's sense. *The Faerie Queene* has nothing like it.

The usual comment that Spenser and Tasso have much in common means, I think, that they are both grave, both Christian, gentle, tender, and without humour. But in the conception and matter of *The Faerie Queene* Spenser was much closer to almost any other of his romance sources than to the *Gerusalemme Liberata*. Even the *Rinaldo* was but one of many writings he must take over into the more complex form Ariosto had perfected, and in the pastoral Spenser could not attempt to explore further the abysses of the *Aminta*.

And yet the old comparison of the two grave poets is still affecting. Perhaps it is the depth of melancholy they seem to know comparably, the tension of disorganization in their most ambitious works, the foreignness of intellectuality to their deepest interests although both were capable of most active and searching thought. And of course the most obvious thing, both were individualists, facing the same problems.

Unity and "The Faerie Queene"

There is much to be said for the conception of unity in variety, that a series of stories with many heroes would by some single conception of the narrator end in the effect of completeness, as if finally all had been said that needed to be. No parsimony would leave us unsatisfied, and there would be so vast a scene, so full a life that we might come to take all this as a view of the world and its richness so magnificent one would not know how to put an end to it.

As if indeed there need not be an end. Just as in *The Shepheardes Calender*, "ending as it began," December being the end to nothing, merely a feature in the arbitrary idea of a calendar, so in an heroic poem the praise of holiness, temperance, chastity, friendship, justice, courtesy, can go on and on, everlastingly changing, and yet all belong to each other much as the months do, passing into and accompanying each other. Any end that would ever be contrived for such praise would also be arbitrary—unless there were a prayer fulfilled, a prayer like Galahad's asking to be transported immediately to Heaven, or like Spenser's own, less ecstatic, that he might see the Sabaoth's sight, or, miraculously, like the final journey that led Brandan to Paradise itself—this the end to the story.

In one sense certainly there can be no end to *The Faerie Queene*. There is no ultimate madness to signify for Spenser as it does for Ariosto the way stories of love will ever end, nor does it all lead to a particular marriage for the definitive comment that can offer, in hope as well as irony. And there can be no end as in Tasso, death of the sort that attends Clorinda or of the kind Godfrey waits for to mark the finish of a pilgrimage. For Tasso as for Ariosto the barrier between the worlds is definite and clear and the story moves between the worlds, and for Tasso human life depends on immortality to fulfil the promises of love. In *The Faerie Queene* there are no barriers between worlds, the realm of the Gods is hardly acknowledged, and it seems it need not be. Since Spenser believes innocence need not be corrupted, for the knights and lovers of his story there need be no finally deferred fulfilments, and all or almost all is contained within one world.

For the success of his poem there needs only to be something like completeness, enough of the sight of questing knights and ladies to make us know the richness of glory and love and innocence, and enough to make us know the complexity of the evils they confront. The poem will create, in short, an image of the richness and variety of the world and of the idea of excellence. All is presented as within the integrity of a vision, and it is the conviction that his vision is whole, that his imagination comprehends all the truths he lives by, that will allow him finally to bring the poem to an end. No event in the story could be other than a conclusion as arbitrary as the naming of December. As in the *Gerusalemme Liberata*, the liberation of Jerusalem is but an incident in the completion of the poem's movement.

So it is that one might expect unity as one begins reading *The Faerie Queene*, not in the conclusion of a series of intertwined adventures but in the attainment of some fullness of meaning and pleasure. Reading the poem this way, the various allegories weave in and out at will, subordinate to the romantic form.

The progress of the Red Crosse Knight was to be through battle and the discipline of contemplation, for in order to perform his mission he was to know the need of purification. Holiness was, indeed, a burden, and there is a hint of this at the very beginning:

> Right faithfull true he was in deede and word,
> But of his cheere did seeme too solemne sad;
> Yet nothing did he dread, but euer was ydrad.
>
> (I. i. 2)

Arthur, although able to come to his aid, was also oppressed, but differently, for his was a "secret wound" (I. ix. 7), but at the time it offered no immediate obstacle to his fighting.

Both these knights in fulfilling their missions, and achieving their virtues, depended on aggression, but Guyon in the deeds of temperance was meeting dangers that were not so much monsters as phantasms, the dreams of the senses, and so his adventures were of a different order than those encountered by Saint George, where the reality of the dragon as of the sacraments needed to be clear. Guyon's chief opponent was neither a devil nor a rival, but a magician, a creator of illusions that the passions feed, and the dangers emphasized the dependence of all virtues on each other, temperance being one state of the life of holiness. So for Guyon there were mostly the vistas of his senses to resist, and his journey became not so much a marching against enemies as a transport through a series of dreams. This passivity contrasts with the aggressions of the Red Crosse Knight and even with the passion felt in the House of Contemplation. The mother of Ruddymane, herself "the image of mortalitie" (II. i. 57), raised the central image of the progress of the knight's life in her protest against God—"sad pageants of mens miseries" (II. i. 36).

Guyon's endurances are often only in the sight of things: of the child playing in his mother's blood; of Furor's fierce attack on Pyrochles; of Mammon's wilderness of wealth. The passivity of his progress is witnessed, too, by this, that more often than the other heroes he is likened to a boat. More than most he is borne on ships, sometimes unaccompanied, sometimes at the mercy of the wind, although the Palmer steered him through the Gulfe of Greedinesse, past the Rock of Vile Reproach and through all the whirlpools. When he arrived at the Bower of Bliss little was required of him as a warrior. There it is as elsewhere—he had known little of the temptation of jealousy that led Phedon to kill his betrothed and his friend; he never gave way to fury, only observed it, unlike the Red Crosse Knight even in this for St. George, hearing the story of Treuisan (I. ix. 37), was himself brought to despair. It is as if the scenes Guyon witnesses are not counterparts of his own struggles, but are only stories to be heard, sights to be seen, imaginings to be believed and avoided. It is the enchantments that need to be undone, and the enchanter (so named, and only so named in this book) who must be avoided.

All this is fitting enough as a stage in the progress of a knight who has first moved towards holiness, and of a gentleman who will in the end combine all virtues. Holiness is about the relations of an individual to the things that are permanent in his life and that in fact transcend it, and love also as Spenser means it is a kind of holiness and it is supported in one way or another by divinity. All must be able to say with Britomart,

> Yet will I not fro mine owne loue remoue.
>
> (III. i. 28)

No magic, no enchantment can remove it—

> But loue, that is in gentle brest begonne,
> No idle charmes so lightly may remoue.
>
> (III. ii. 51)

If there are times when in some lover it may be well called a sacred fire—

> Most sacred fire, that burnest mightily
> In liuing brests, ykindled first aboue,
> Emongst th'eternall spheres and lamping sky—
>
> (III. iii. 1)

at least one other time it is the very instrument of Providence

> It was not, *Britomart*, thy wandring eye,
> Glauncing vnwares in charmed looking glas,
> But the streight course of heauenly destiny,
> Led with eternall prouidence, that has
> Guided thy glaunce, to bring his will to pas.
>
> (III. iii. 24)

So there is the long genealogy of Arthur and that of Britomart to show us how divinity entered history, along with Timias's *Dea certe*! (III. v. 35). And there is the wonderful symbolism of Chrysogone, conceiving of the rays of the sun.

Friendship, too, or whatever one calls the love of the soul in contrast to that of the body (IV. ix. 2) is another means of stability, comparable to the use of temperance, for love must always be the love of virtue or else its sovereign power would turn to waste:

O soueraigne Lord that sit'st on hye,
And raignst in blis emongst thy blessed Saintes,
How suffrest thou such shamefull cruelty,
So long vnwreaked of thine enimy?
Or hast thou, Lord, of good mens cause no heed?
Or doth thy iustice sleepe, and silent ly?
What booteth then the good and righteous deed,
If goodnesse find no grace, nor righteousness no meed?

(III. xi. 9)

Friendship and kinship together with the attachments of love lead to all those matters where it is seen that justice is necessary for the health of society, so there is reason that the story of such as Arthegall should follow now in the list of the virtues of a gentleman. His life of course is the most active of all, and as the most warlike it is perhaps to be expected that he should be the one most violently overcome by love. Only with him as the agent of justice it is more clear than with the others that his adventures can never reach an end. Communism is overcome, the Catholics of Spain defeated, Ireland is restored to peace, Mercy is established with Justice—the mere enumeration suggests all that is yet to do.

And if, to follow the accretion of such virtues one were to suppose there should be a necessity for a book of Courtesy, it would be perhaps because one needs always to return to some other way of looking at purity of motive, at the beginnings of holiness—

vertues seat is deepe within the mynd.

(Proem to Book VI. v)

The life of the just as that of the lover and the temperate must always keep touch with that inborn perfection that justifies our hope to know about holiness, and that will always guide us to know that temperance and love and justice are the inheritance of humans—

Whose euery deed and word, that he did say,
Was like enchantment, that through both the eyes,
And both the eares did steale the hart away.

(VI. ii. 3)

Like as the gentle hart it selfe bewrayes,
 In doing gentle deedes with franke delight.
(VI. vii. 1)

 For seldome yet did liuing creature see,
That curtesie and manhood euer disagree.
(VI. iii. 40)

So it is, I think, that one may say of the books of *The Faerie Queene*, that their succession is devised to present with some fullness an image of the variety of the world, showing first that kind of glory called holiness, and then such other matters as belong to those of "glorious great intent." And it is as important to repeat as it is to add, all virtues being forms of each other.

Bishop Hurd's discussion of the unity of *The Faerie Queene* is one of the most fruitful that has been offered.

If you ask then, what is this *Unity* of Spenser's Poem? I say, it consists in the relation of its several adventures to one common *original*, the appointment of the *Fairy Queen*; and to one common *end*, the completion of the Fairy Queen's injunctions. The knights issued forth on their adventures on the breaking up of this annual feast: and the next annual feast, we are to suppose, is to bring them together again from the atchievement of their several charges.

This, it is true, is not the classic Unity which consists in the representation of one entire action: but it is an Unity of another sort, an unity resulting from the respect which a number of related actions have to one common purpose. In other words, it is an unity of *design*, and not of action.

This *Gothic* method of design in poetry may be, in some sort, illustrated by what is called the *Gothic* method of design in gardening. A wood or grove cut out into many separate avenues or glades was among the most favourite of the works of art, which our fathers attempted in this species of cultivation. These walks were distinct from each other, had each their several destination, and terminated on their own proper objects. Yet the whole was brought together and considered under one view, by the relation which these various openings had, not to each other, but to their common and concurrent centre.[1]

[1] *Letters on Chivalry and Romance*, Letter VIII, in *The Works of Richard Hurd*, London, 1811, IV, 300–301.

One may not agree with Hurd's conception of the function of Arthur, and there are still other matters to question,[1] but the point he made about "design" is instructive, particularly when attention is given to the supporting idea included in the words, "the whole was brought together and considered under one view." This throws the question of unity back upon the purposes of the poet, and by such a suggestion Hurd avoids treating design as a form of unity with an existence of its own.

In the history of criticism there have been similar efforts to characterize the unity of works whose structure is more or less like that of *The Faerie Queene*, and some of these are of help in studying Spenser and Hurd both.

The late Professor Pauphilet in writing on the thirteenth-century *Queste del Saint Graal* called attention to its innovations. Until this work, he said, the poets and writers of romances had been telling of a single hero pursuing his adventures. The author of this romance introduced the conception of a general quest in which all the knights of the Round Table participated. "Innovation féconde, et qui, par une bizarre fortune, après avoir heureusement renouvelé l'antique légende du Graal, a fini par la tuer. Car l'élargissement de la quête était le moyen de montrer plusieurs types d'âme à la recherche de Dieu; c'était le moyen de faire sortir du thème traditionnel, au lieu d'un roman biographique, un tableau vaste et varié comme la chrétienté même."[2]

To explain how such a way of telling a story might still give the effect of unity he made a comparison with Gothic windows, and if this is an analogy not easily pursued in a rational way there still remains the fact, the perfection of the beauty of such an achievement: "La *Queste* est ordonnée comme la décoration d'un édifice religieux. Elle ressemble à ces grandes verrières de Chartres dont les multiples médaillons ne font qu'un seul sujet; dissemblables en apparence, tous les motifs ont au fond la même signification,

[1] W. L. Renwick has given a fine outline of Renaissance theories on the kinds of poetry in order to show how Spenser's poem follows some of their prescriptions on unity (*Edmund Spenser*, London, 1925, pp. 46–55).

[2] Albert Pauphilet, *Études sur La Queste del Saint Graal*, Paris, 1921, p. 120.

comme ils ont les mêmes couleurs: ce sont les nuances d'une seule idée; pour l'esprit comme pour le regard, leur diversité se fond en une riche unité et leur enseignement est harmonieux comme leur lumière."[1]

Professor Mario Casella's theories concerning the unity of romances, developed most fully in his study of *Don Quixote*, go so far in the defence of "Gothic unity" that he risks the criticism of a special plea for the truth of a particular philosophy, Augustinianism. Up to that point, however, his ideas agree well enough with cooler criticism and are indeed remarkable.

In the works of Dante, Chrétien, Ariosto, and Cervantes, he argues, there exists a unity that bears analogy to metaphysical unity, "a rational truth that gradually takes shape and comes to light as the profound purpose presiding over the composition of the work and that becomes clear in the complex harmony of the whole. Episodes and stories are bound up together according to some likeness to each other, and according to some likeness—it is never identical—to the central narration.

"We thus have an art that seeks out differences in the midst of similarities, careful to point to the individual rather than the generic; but this 'individual,' this thing in itself (*vere ens, vere unum*), reveals always universal characteristics, by virtue of which it may be inserted (retaining its own unity) with the vast, intellligible unity of the whole work. And this explains why an individual *novella*, autonomous in itself, may be suppressed without doing harm to the purpose that governs the composition in all its complexity, or without damaging the continuity of the central exposition.

Lasciate questo canto, che senza esso
puo star l'istoria e non sara men chiara—
(XXVIII. 2)

[Let this canto go, for the story will stand
without it and not be any less clear]—

[1] Albert Pauphilet, *Études sur La Queste del Saint Graal*, Paris, 1921, p. 169.

says Ariosto as he is about to insert into his poem the *novella* of *Giocondo* and *Astolfo*. . . ."[1]

In the view of Professor Giuseppe Toffanin, Ariosto's successive redactions of the *Furioso* were undertaken in order to reconcile a conflict between certain religious and chivalric interests that showed a weakness in the initial conception. His main point is that the harmony of the four chief stories—the madness of Orlando, the wedding of Ruggiero and Bradamante, the knightly adventures of the paladins, and the fight against the infidels—is a forced one because Ariosto was unable to unify his religious and chivalric interests even in subduing them to his humour.[2]

All these critics agree, I think, in accepting the romances they write of as compositions of a primarily individual forming, their structure derived in the very beginning from the particular interests of the poet, his temperament and his way of imagining or dreaming. Professor Casella, however, means to extend his argument to account for "the spirit of romance," in Ezra Pound's phrase, and so to account for a community of interest in so many imaginative endeavours. Except for a certain sophistication of philosophy in his reasoning, all these ideas appear to have been part of the great debates in Italy in the sixteenth century, and Tasso's own arguing comprehends, I think, the substantial matters of these later discussions.

He expressed his primary conception of the unity of romances in his superb discussion of "variety": "Variety is to be praised up to that point where it would pass into confusion, and unity can contain variety within a little of that same limit. As Boethius says, plurality, when it is not the primary condition, is accidental to unity. If Variety, presented as such, is not present in a poem of a single action, one is more likely to believe that this is a lack of skill in the artist rather than a defect in the art, even though artists in order to excuse their inadequacy may ascribe faults to the art that more truly represent their own failings. It seems that variety was

[1] *Cervantes, Il Chisciotte*, 2 vols., Florence: Le Monnier, 1938, I, 89. Professor Casella also has certain obligations to Schelling (see J.-J. A. Bertrand, *Cervantes et le Romantisme Allemand*, Paris, 1914, pp. 189–201).

[2] *Il Cinquecento*, 3rd edition, Milan: Vallardi, 1945, pp. 196–97.

not so necessary in the times of Virgil and Homer, for the taste of the men of those times was not so satiated as to require it. These poets, therefore, did not attain variety, although more is to be found in Virgil than in Homer. In our own time variety has afforded the greatest pleasure, and because of this our poets have been obliged to flavour their poems with the spice of variety, not wanting to fail those of the most refined taste. If there have been some who have not tried to manage this, it is either because they failed to see the need of it, or else they despaired of its possibility. For my part I judge it a most pleasing thing in an heroic poem, and that it is possible to arrange. For just as one sees in the marvellous dominion of God that is called the world such a variety of stars scattered over the sky and adorning it, and as one looks from these into the lower parts of the universe, passing from one region to another, the air and the sea full of birds and fish, and the earth host to so many animals both wild and tame and where there are streams and fountains and lakes and meadows and fields and woods and mountains, here fruits and flowers, there snow and ice, here dwellings and cultivated land, there solitudes and wastes, and although the world includes so many and such various things in its bosom its form and its essence are one, and there is one knot which gathers together and binds its parts, from discord into harmony. ... The poem that includes so great a variety of matter is no less one in form and in soul, and all its elements are put together in such a way that one is related to another, one corresponds to another, one depends on another either necessarily or apparently, so that if one part is taken away, or if its position is changed, all is destroyed. And if this is true, the art of composing the poem is like the principle of the universe, which goes by contraries, like the principle of music, for if there were no multiplicity, there would be no whole and no law, as Plotinus says."[1]

[1] "... dico bene, che la varietá è lodevole sino a quel termine che non passi in confusione; e per poco l'unitá n'è capace sino a questo termine istesso; perché a l'unitá, che non è la prima, è accidentale, come dice Boezio, la moltitudine; e se la diversitá sí fatta non si vede in poema d'una azione, si dee credere che sia piú tosto imperizia de gli artefici, che difetto de l'arte, i quali, per

Donadoni observed that the unity of the *Liberata* exists in the "lyrical impulsion" that is the occasion of the work and that continues throughout.[1] All this that Tasso thinks of as an imitation of multiplicity is brought together by this initial passion, an enthusiasm that is always being kindled and always sovereign. In his own criticism Tasso would give warrant for this observation, I think, in his many remarks on the relation of poetry to truth. One of them goes like this: "The subject of an Epic Poem should be taken from the history of true religion, but a part not so sacred it is immutable, and from a period neither too remote nor too close in memory to the time in which we are now living."[2] And

iscusare forse la loro insofficienza, questa lor propria colpa attribuiscono a l'arteficio. Non era peraventura cosí necessaria questa varietá a' tempi di Vergilio e d'Omero, essendo gli uomini di quel secolo di gusto non cosí isvogliato; però non tanto v'attesero: maggiore nondimeno in Virgilio che in Omero si ritrova. Gratissima era a' nostri tempi; e perciò dovevano i nostri poeti co' sapori di questa varietá condire i loro poemi, volendo che da questi gusti sí delicati non fossero schivati: e s'alcuni non tentarono d'introdurlavi, o non conobbero il bisogno, o il disperarono come impossibile. Io e soavissima nel poema eroico la stimo, e possibile a conseguire: peroché, sí come in questo mirabile magisterio di Dio, che mondo si chiama, e 'l cielo si vede sparso o distinto di tanta varietá di stelle, e, discendendo poi giú di regione in regione, l'aria e 'l mare pieni di ucelli e di pesci, e la terra albergatrice di tanti animali cosí feroci, come mansueti, ne la quale e ruscelli e fonti e laghi e prati e campagne e selve e monti sogliamo rimirare, e qui frutti e fiori, lá ghiacci e nevi, qui abitazioni e culture, lá solitudine ed orrori; con tutto ciò uno è il mondo che tante e sí diverse cose nel suo grembo rinchiude, una la forma e l'essenza sua, uno il nodo dal quale sono le sue parti con discorde concordia insieme congiunte e collegate; . . . ma che nondimeno uno sia il poema che tanta varietá di materie contegna, una la forma e l'anima sua, e che tutte queste cose sieno di maniera composte, che l'una l'altra riguardi, l'una a l'altra corrisponda, l'una da l'altra o necessariamente o verisimilmente dependa, sí che una sola parte o tolta via, o mutata di sito, il tutto si distrugga. E se ciò fosse vero, l'arte del comporre il poema sarebbe simile a la ragion de l'universo, la qual è composta de' contrari, come la ragion musica: perché s'ella non fosse moltiplice, non sarebbe tutta, né sarebbe ragione, come dice Plotino." "Discorsi del Poema Eroico," in *Prose*, ed. Francesco Flora, Milan, 1935, pp. 411–13.

[1] Eugenio Donadoni, *Torquato Tasso*, 3rd edition, Florence: 1946, pp. 177–78.

[2] *Discorsi del Signor Torquato Tasso. Dell' Arte Poetica; et in particolare del Poema Heroico*, Venice, 1587, p. 6.

although the appeal is not merely to truth but to true religion, Donadoni, pressing the point of Tasso's similarity to later romantics, is interpreting fairly enough when he takes Tasso to mean that the heroic poet may also be concerned with "an opinion of the truth."[1]

Whatever the impulsion or inspiration that controls variety and gives it the form of unity, the experience of the reader can alone justify such claims as Tasso and indeed the later critics make in this regard. The test of memory that Tasso offered is an interesting one, partly because it probably depends on the same line of Neo-Platonism as his argument for variety: "That poem is extremely pleasing in which the reader's memory never gets lost or confused, when it can take in all as a unit and can consider how one thing is connected to another and one depends on another and how the parts are proportioned among themselves and to the whole. Without any doubt those poems are faulty, and the work in them has been wasted, where when the reader has gone a little past the middle he finds that he has forgotten the beginning. Then, indeed, the very delight is lost which the poet ought to strive to achieve most zealously as his principal perfection. The perfect aim is realized when one event follows another either of necessity or probability, when each event is part of a single chain and not to be separated, as when from an elaborate weaving of knots there is devised an intrinsic, probable and unexpected solution. If by chance anyone should consider the *Innamoramento* and the *Furioso* as a single poem its very length would very likely be excessive, and so it would not be likely to be held in the simple reading of an ordinary memory."[2]

[1] *Torquato Tasso*, p. 134.

[2] "Grande è conueneuolmente quel Poema, in cui la memoria non si perde nè si smarisce, ma tutto unitamente comprehendendolo, può considerare come l'una cosa con l'altra sia connessa, e dall' altra dependa, e come le parti frà loro e co'l tutto siano proportionate. Vitiosi sono senza dubbio que' Poemi, & in buona parte perduta è l'opera, che ui si spende, ne' quali di poco hà il Lettore passato il mezo, che del principio si è dimenticato, peroche ui si perde quel diletto, che dal Poeta come principale perfettione deue essere con ogni studio ricercato. Questo è come l'uno auuenimento doppo l'altro necessariamente, ò uerisimilmente succeda, come l'uno con l'altro sia concatenato, e dall'altro

The sequence of events in the *Gerusalemme Liberata* is unforgettable, although this cannot be for the mere reason of logical continuity. But when we read the *Orlando Furioso* and *The Faerie Queene*, we are convinced that it would be no use to try to recall what had happened earlier if we were only to rely on some natural organization of our attention and the power of the poetry. To remember most of *The Faerie Queene* we should need to leave our reading in order to force the incidents of the early scenes to mind again. It is such a fact that has led some readers to declare that far from being a poem this is only a collection of stanzas.

And yet there is a mistake here, of course, in part because our attention is cumulatively rewarded independently of the remembrance of details in themselves and independently of an idea of a continuing logic in the action. If we are concentrating on the narrative and we are regarding the various allegories as subordinate and discontinuous, the major patterns are never obscured: the different heroes are simple, not complex, all are phrases of one hero, the stakes are always the highest, the goal is always love and glory, innocence is at the heart of the suspense, the marvellous is the end. Free from the insinuations of sustained allegory we accept the contrasts of Books I and II as contrasts, and the interwoven stories of Books III and IV as a continuing enrichment, and when we come to V and VI we are quite content they should be composed as they are. And I think we can agree with Bishop Hurd that all together these offer the pleasures of variety and harmony, from a certain point of view. We demand only that the conditions of the fantastic prevail, that nothing be done to destroy the charm of that, or interrupt us from exploring what the love of the far away, the note of marvel and yearning, means to us who are outside the scene, and that nothing distract our concern for the knight and lover whose aspiration carries the burdens of constancy and

inseparabile, & in somma come da una artificiosa testurà de' nodi nasca una intrinseca e uerisimile, & inespettata solutione, e per auentura chi l'Innamoramento e'l Furioso, come un solo Poema considerasse gli potria parere la sua lunghezza souerchia, anzi che nò, & non atta ad esser contenuta in una simplice lettione da una mediocre memoria." (*Discorsi del Signor Torquato Tasso*, p. 13).

holiness. What we should require most of all is repetition, the sounding again of the same wonderful changes:

> Wonder it is to see, in diuerse minds—
> The noble hart, that harbours vertuous thought—

that, and the promise that some time in the narrative there should be a rounding off of the questing, some final, significant relation of the romantic yearning to the narrator's own impulsion. As the marriage of Ruggiero and Bradamante for Ariosto, and as for Tasso the defeat of Armida, the apotheosis of Clorinda, and the conquest of Jerusalem, so for Spenser we hope for some event to be the flower of the whole of the poem. We have been led so far in meditation on the ideas of chivalry and of pastoral innocence that we expect Spenser's conception of their power to be summed up in an event or image towards which the whole poem will be known to have moved.

As things turned out, the poem unfinished, it is difficult to see how this might have been done. But the fragment of the *Book of Constancie* gives such emphasis to a conception that is surely fundamental to the whole work, that it raises the final question—are the methods and subjects of *The Faerie Queene* controlled by some such single purpose and attitude as the *Liberata*, and perhaps the *Furioso?*

Mutability gets her hearing before Nature on Arlo-Hill, once a place for Diana to take joy in, and now, as all the earth, abandoned by the gods. Yet it is, one must suppose, as beautiful as ever, as loved of all others as ever. And Mutability's plea is superb, clear, simple, beautiful, true. Air, earth, fire, water are continually becoming each other, and not merely is the substance of things always changing, there is time itself in its motion, the seasons, the months, days and hours, Day and Night, all are constantly passing into each other just as Death passes into Life and Life into Death. All this that changes so is so beautiful that Jove himself whose own rule is threatened by it is also charmed and enamoured, and he finds he cannot use violence against the Titan. But he at least asserts himself to claim that he and the other gods are sovereign over time, and this although Mutability has reminded him that no dynasty, even of the gods, is eternal.

If he cannot make his claim quite meaningful, Nature can. She says that all change is but the way towards perfection, and when all fulfilments are achieved there shall be rest, changelessness, eternally. She means that to the thought of mortals change can only be understood by reference to the idea of changelessness, and that the complaint against change and mortality comes from those who dream of constancy and immortality. She means, too, that the great motions of the universe itself as of the changes of seasons come from some stillness at the heart of things, a peace beyond the universe.

It is the knowledge of constancy that makes us complain of change, because we believe that the end of aspiration, rest, is also that from which we come. Such is indeed the origin of Nature, of all the gods, of the universe, of all that is mutable.

When the great argument is over, the remarkable intellectuality completed, the poem returns to Spenser who speaks in his own person, as if he himself were present at the assembly of the gods on Arlo-Hill, listening to Nature. And he adds what only a human could, and what reason and philosophy and the tremendous argument could not, the passion of faith, faith aspiring to translation, and a statement that includes a new renunciation of the too-much loved earth. The praise of constancy has now become the explicit Christian beseeching, and all that Pastorella and her life had once meant of perfection in the universe is unremembered.

In its expression of religion this is as profound as any poetry in English, and however extended *The Faerie Queene* should be it could not have carried a meaning to go beyond this. But here the key has changed from what was dominant before, and that which was once the praise of constancy in the desire for glory and in love is now the constancy of a man alone praying to God. The single singer of chivalry is now an individual in prayer, and the world of Faerie Land and all that it contains is put aside for the thought of the Sabaoth's sight. All is transmuted, another Paradise has become the substance of the vision, and the vision is the sight of another reality. The scene is no longer the romantic world; nor is it a world of such dreams as come to Arthur of Glorianne, and it is unlike the magic mirror in which Britomart could see prophetically. This is the Vision of Paradise, and of Judgment, forever contradicting the merely imagined world.

Having come to such a place in his thought and given it expression in *The Faerie Queene*, it is difficult to see how Spenser could look back upon the other books of the poem and see them as part of a conception leading to these cantos. It is equally difficult to see, how, after such a statement, he could have included in the poem the adventures of still other knights, and gone on to the final story of Arthur's magnificence. In his own prayer for peace he has expressed an intransigent interest in the world of the gods, beings who had been of so little consequence to the rest of the poem, and in the *Mutabilitie* cantos all that remains of the original conception is the image of the solitary poet with his initial trust.[1]

For a while, in the Book of Courtesy, the gods had come upon the scene in the story of the miraculous birth of Belphoebe and Amoret. There was also the story of the disappearance of Cupid for whom Venus had gone in search. After a while she met up with Diana and when they got over their strangeness they joined in the search together and in time came upon the two infants. Once in a story about Arlo-Hill we are told about Diana and the Faun, once about Astraea and her departure from the earth, although as persons these are not active in the poem, and there are brief stories about Morpheus and some others. The story of Marinell is the only one in an elaborately mythological context although the mythological suggestions are rich in the scene showing the graces as they circle the maiden to whom Colin is devoted. They dance

[1] C. S. Lewis as usual has written very interestingly on the *Mutabilitie* cantos, and especially, it seems to me, about their religiousness. He refers, too, to Spenser's decision not to bring God on the stage, so to speak, and this he indicates has medieval analogies and is a sign of a deeper religiousness in *The Faerie Queene* than *Paradise Lost* can claim. (*The Allegory of Love*, London: Oxford University Press, 1948, pp. 354–5.) But, unfortunately, he does not develop the matter. Renwick gives a useful summary of the ideas of Cinthio and some others on the use of mythology in epic poetry (*Edmund Spenser*, pp. 142–6).

about her as they would in serving Venus, and we are reminded by the scene itself as by her charm that Pastorella is indeed like a goddess, her quality is divine and she herself has such strength she can survive the terrible invasion and massacre unchanged.

In this matter *The Faerie Queene* differs greatly from the manner of *Orlando Furioso* and the *Gerusalemme Liberata*. In Ariosto's poem the land of the gods is some starry palace in the heavens, and from there on occasion God sends His messengers to Ferrara or Himself speaks to those at the court. In Tasso's poem, angels come to the battlefield, the spirit of a dead woman takes up her life in Heaven, and there are many like incidents. In these the worlds of the imagination and of faith are mingled. Until the *Mutabilitie* cantos Spenser had forgone the opportunities of such a conception, and any continuation of *The Faerie Queene* could not have introduced the gods into the action of a knight like Arthur in a design that would be harmonious to the scene already given unless they were to play a minor part.

In Malory as in *La Queste del Saint Graal* deaths or true visions could supply the completion of the pattern, but such reality or vividness is alien to the conception of *The Faerie Queene*, and when a vision is spoken of in the *Mutabilitie* cantos the poem becomes instead of a narrative a hymn. Yet paradoxically it is the nature of the previous commitments to the beauty of mortality that make the last prayer a return to the poetic representation of the solitary singer. Had they depended on a Platonism that was at all rigorous, there might have been as in the *Phaedo* a final affirmation of immortality that philosophy and allegory would support, and without the desperation of the last lines. Had the allegory been conceived integrally with the romance form, as in the *Queste*, all might have culminated in some such image as the Vision of Er in the *Republic*. But Spenser's strength came from the simpler commitments of nature, from the beauty and wisdom that belonged to the simple shepherd, taking the good of life as it came, forming himself by what he loved, Rosalind, the earth the sea, light. There was as life went on room for regret, in the Du Bellay term, for time destroyed all, and so he would allow his imagination to desire the return of the Golden Age. The acts of his mind that he would call visions also taught him about the corrupting power of time, of glories no longer on the earth.

For such a man the sense of constancy is as it were a fact of nature, and a recognition of nature, the state of innocence like that in which Calidore saw the Graces dancing. It depended, too, on an informing principle he believed to exist within variety itself, a quality in change that was somehow not destructive. The procession of time itself conformed to a pattern of constancy, the months of the year, the hours of the day that led to the poet's marriage, the succession of journeys beginning at Gloriana's court, all relating to the changing forms of life that reveal an abiding life and truth.[1] But the philosophical or even the religious interpretation of such beliefs, even when Spenser himself offers them in comment or allegory, are an inexact substitute for what is only to be spoken of properly as a perception or an affirmation. These are not so much ideas as the loyalties of nature, and the words he uses express simply the disposition of the mind to wonder.

If the decay of splendour is equally an affirmation never to be denied, it is not inevitable that a poet should do as Spenser does in protesting against the wastes of time, develop stories of the romantic quest in the indefinite past towards the imaginary restoration of the sway of innocence. But this is one way of reconciling what one

[1] Miss Kathleen Williams seems to me to have made by far the best study of the unity of Spenser's conception in her essay, "'Eterne in Mutabilitie': The Unified World of *The Faerie Queene*" (in *That Soueraine Light, Essays in Honor of Edmund Spenser*, 1552–1952, eds. William R. Mueller and Don Cameron Allen, Baltimore: Johns Hopkins Press, 1952, pp. 35–50). Part of her most thoughtful discussion is summarized in these words: ". . . the latest and fullest of such unifying passages as these is to be found in the fragment *Of Mutability*, a more explicit statement of the great theme which earlier books express chiefly by symbol and by arrangement of material. These two cantos, and the two final stanzas, are the culmination of the poem as it now stands, both unifying and illuminating it. Spenser's description of Nature, and Mutability's address to her, show her as the source—or rather as nearest to that source which man may know—of the conceptions in other books. She embodies Justice and Concord, she is veiled like Venus, and by her likeness to the transfigured Christ she suggests the Holiness of Book I. Mutability, on the other hand, is Corruption, sin, or the consequences of sin as seen in our world." (P. 48.) In this she is partly going on from C. S. Lewis in *The Allegory of Love*.

might most need to reconcile, the knowledge of the importance of love and the fact of the passing of time. *The Faerie Queene* is thus in part the effort of the poet to reckon with many of the changes chance brings in the course of time, and to work it out so that it can be seen that those first perceptions of the pastoral beauty of things shall justify the love it occasioned, so that somehow the world of Pastorella and the Graces shall be known to be eternal.

The fidelities of a poet though now and then related to philosophy mean more for all his work than ideas ever can. As if, as a child, some perception took form, and the rest of life meant weighing and guiding all experience and all expression by that first wonderful acceptance. And more than that, as if, as a poet, no matter how life and civilization crowd him with words and styles his work can only prosper as that first truth of his is followed.

For Spenser the loyalty, the perception that can from time to time accept ideas is the knowledge of constancy, and what this means is the constancy of excellence, and what one must by the very nature of the choices of life be faithful to. The beauty of Rosalind, the gaiety of April, the innocence of love, the pride of glory and the love of holiness, their claims are all one and complete. Their power enslaves the rest, the growing sum of experience, and all that time teaches us about change, about inconstancy, decay, death, and all that the mind does to relate these terrible things, to help us discover the coherence of appearances, cannot ever lead to the denial of that first love, that reality his being moved towards by instinct. That moving of the mind towards truth, that instinctive gesture of the body is the proof of what it affirms:

> For loue is Lord of truth and loialtie.
>
> (*Hymne of Love*, 176)

The lasting acceptance of pastoral forms meant that Spenser's nature, his mind, could never turn from the notion of the incorruptibility of innocence, but in the *Mutabilitie* cantos, where the prayer carries so rich a sense of the defeat of the Christian, of weariness with the world, there is also wonder at an order of reality known to nothing but faith, faith in another world and another life.[1] In the romance itself, although the sense of the divine is everywhere, the gods themselves do not appear.

[1] Mr. W. C. B. Watkins has argued that Spenser's "affirmation of the spiritual" here is unconvincing (*Shakespeare & Spenser*, Princeton: Princeton University Press, 1950, p. 72). "These two final stanzas of the *Mutabilitie* cantos are moving precisely because they express humble and suppliant prayer, desire rather than affirmation." But prayer, of course, can include affirmation, and even in Saint Paul the necessities and weaknesses of desire cannot be said to undo his faith. I think Mr. Watkins' analysis here is also neglectful of the majesty of these lines, which is surely important in any consideration of the question of their spiritual affirmation.

INDEX

For Product Safety Concerns and Information please contact our EU representative GPSR@taylorandfrancis.com
Taylor & Francis Verlag GmbH, Kaufingerstraße 24, 80331 München, Germany

www.ingramcontent.com/pod-product-compliance
Lightning Source LLC
Chambersburg PA
CBHW070537100726
47907CB00004B/1155

* 9 7 8 1 0 3 2 8 3 3 5 7 6 *